essential brakhage

Selected Writings on Filmmaking

by Stan Brakhage

Edited with a foreword
by Bruce R. McPherson

DOCUMENTEXT 2001

ESSENTIAL BRAKHAGE

Published by McPherson & Company, Post Box 1126, Kingston, New York 12402. Publication of this book has been assisted by a grant from the Literature Program of the New York State Council on the Arts. Design by Bruce R. McPherson. First edition. First printing June 2001.

1 3 5 7 9 10 8 6 4 2   2001 2002 2003 2004 2005

Library of Congress Cataloging-in-Publication Data

Brakhage, Stan.
   Essential Brakhage : selected writings on filmmaking / by Stan
Brakhage ; edited with a foreword by Bruce R. McPherson.
     p.   cm.
   Includes bibliographical references.
   ISBN 0-929701-64-X ✓
   1. Motion pictures—Philosophy. I. McPherson, Bruce R. (Bruce Rice), 1951-
   II. Title.

PN1995.B716 2001
791.43'01—dc21

                                                           2001030956

Selections from *Metaphors on Vision,* copyright © 1963 by Film Culture, Inc., are reprinted courtesy of Film Culture, Inc. and the author. Some other material in this volume previously appeared, occasionally in slightly different form, in the following magazines and journals: *Dartmouth, Guerilla, Cinema Now, Harbinger, Dance Perspectives, Io, Filmmakers Newsletter, Criss-Cross Communications, credences,* and *Millennium Film Journal.* "A Moving Picture Giving and Taking Book" was originally published by Frontier Press, copyright © 1971 by Stan Brakhage. "The Seen" first appeared from Pasteurize Press as a small pamphlet, copyright © 1975 by Stan Brakhage.

Stan Brakhage's films are available for rental or purchase from Canyon Cinema (2325 Third St., Ste. 338, San Francisco, CA 94107) and Film-makers' Cooperative (c/o The Clocktower Gallery, 108 Leonard St., 13th floor, New York, NY 10013).

contents

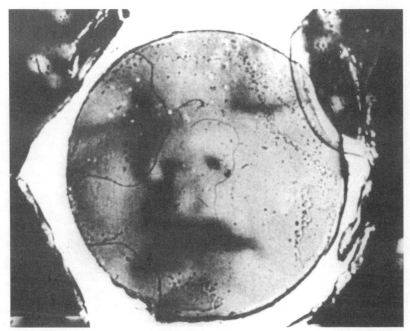

Dog Star Man

foreword

Throughout the fifty years that Stan Brakhage has been forging one of the more compelling bodies of work of any living visual artist—nearly 350 independently produced, innovative films of every description, ranging in length from a few seconds to several hours—he has been carrying on a parallel, somewhat informal, but no less serious discourse in the form of theoretical and historical essays, lectures, personal correspondence, manifestos, and program notes and annotations published in film, literary and art magazines. Much of this has been collected as well in a variety of books. Few artists, let alone filmmakers, have managed so engagingly discursive a critique of their art (and craft). And for decades the writings of Stan Brakhage have held a special appeal to a broad audience of readers beyond or in addition to students of film, and not simply as purported glimpses into the mental proceedings of a "genius," or as skeleton keys to the ciphers and intentions underlying particular films.

Into any discussion of film art Brakhage is likely to draw the poetics of William Blake, Gertrude Stein, and Charles Olson; to invoke the philosophy of Johannes Scotus Erigena; to cite the paintings of Monet and Cezanne, or the music of Bach, Varèse or Tenney; and he does so without being academic. His writing, like his film aesthetic, is rather unique. For Brakhage, film necessarily intersects other arts—poetry, music, painting, sculpture, even mathematics—however much it must also be regarded as an art unto itself. He believes that those intersections present film with its greatest potential to step beyond the conventional form of fictional entertainment, by connecting film to a rich intellectual and aesthetic lineage. Brakhage's conception of film might be said, at one extreme, to extend toward a transcendental or Romantic ideal of Imagination to be attained in a quest for insight. At the other extreme, visual phenomenology itself provides a fertile, literal territory for exploration through film, even down to the emotive and psychodynamic processes beneath the physical experience of vision. The shifting space between these poles is the film art created by the artist.

Likewise, Stan Brakhage cannot be said to be an "easy" writer in the sense that he revels in the polyvalence of language and perceives metaphor at the root of all human understanding: early on he warns that "...I deck my prose with whatever puns come my way, aiming at deliberate ambiguity, hoping thereby to create a disbelief in the rigidity of any linguistic statement, knowing only poetry immortal enough to escape the rigorous belief in any one word-world as a sense-killing finality...."

Essential Brakhage is conceived as an entry point to the viewing and study of the films, which are the truly essential work (and pleasure). This assemblage of writings consists mainly of material from *Metaphors on Vision* (1963) and *Brakhage Scrapbook* (1982)—the principal collections of theoretical texts—supplemented by three pieces from the 1990s. Both books cited have been out of print for a considerable time*; on the secondhand market they are rare and usually quite expensive. These were compilations also, though P. Adams Sitney's editing of *Metaphors on Vision* rendered a relatively seamless text; I have drawn roughly from the first half of that book. The texts selected from *Brakhage Scrapbook* (as Robert Haller first edited them), appear more or less chronologically, offer relatively fewer linguistic challenges, and demonstrate Brakhage's later growth as an artist.

In making this selection of writings I have sought to include at least one representative example of each form of Brakhage

---

The Beaubourg Museum, Paris, publishes a French edition of Metaphors on Vision.

text: manifesto, rough note, pre-screening lecture, post-screening Q&A, shooting scenario, narrative script, poem, and theoretical essay. To make manifest Brakhage's sense of the relationships between film and other arts, and those between himself and other artists, was a particular concern. Unfortunately, his correspondence, while abundant in both of the source books, could not be included here for reasons of space: this text could easily have occupied four or five hundred pages. However, the letters tend to elaborate upon issues and ideas whose outlines are well represented here. *Essential Brakhage* is not intended to supplant the earlier volumes, after all, but to provide new audiences a groundwork to approach the films and additional books. Film students in particular will wish to consult R. Bruce Elder's remarkable study, *The Films of Stan Brakhage in the American Tradition of Ezra Pound, Gertrude Stein, and Charles Olson*, alongside P. Adams Sitney's classic *Visionary Film* (OUP, 1979).

Selected annotations by Brakhage to various films (through 2000) are printed as an appendix; here again the items chosen exhibit the range of Brakhage's descriptive strategies but do not reflect or presume a hierarchy of any sort. Notes to some important films not included were too cursory to be of use, or are nonexistent. And during the 1990s Brakhage's films were largely hand-painted abstractions—visually powerful experiences which literally defy description: One or two annotations stand for all.

I wish to thank Marilyn Jull Brakhage for supplying an up-to-date selected bibliography to augment the 1983 standard reference, *Stan Brakhage: A Guide to References and Resources* by Gerald R. Barrett and Wendy Brabner. Bob Haller and P. Adams Sitney have my gratitude for their encouragement and gentle direction in this undertaking. Anthology Film Archives kindly provided a number of film stills for reproduction.

This book is dedicated to my children, Aaron and Alyssa, who remind me daily of the need for constant revisioning.

—*Bruce R. McPherson, April 26, 2001*

metaphors
on vision

Text of Light

metaphors on vision

Imagine an eye unruled by man-made laws of perspective, an eye unprejudiced by compositional logic, an eye which does not respond to the name of everything but which must know each object encountered in life through an adventure of perception. How many colors are there in a field of grass to the crawling baby unaware of "Green"? How many rainbows can light create for the untutored eye? How aware of variations in heat waves can that eye be? Imagine a world alive with incomprehensible objects and shimmering with an endless variety of movement and innumerable gradations of color. Imagine a world before the "beginning was the word."

To see is to retain—to behold. Elimination of all fear is in sight—which must be aimed for. Once vision may have been given—that which seems inherent in the infant's eye, an eye which reflects the loss of innocence more eloquently than any other human feature, an eye which soon learns to classify sights, an eye which mirrors the movement of the individual toward death by its increasing inability to see.

But one can never go back, not even in imagination. After the loss of innocence, only the ultimate of knowledge can balance the wobbling pivot. Yet I suggest that there is a pursuit of knowledge foreign to language and founded upon visual communication, demanding a development of the optical mind, and dependent upon perception in the original and deepest sense of the word.

Suppose the Vision of the saint and the artist to be an increased ability to see—vision. Allow so-called hallucination to enter the realm of perception, allowing that mankind always finds derogatory terminology for that which doesn't appear to be readily usable, accept dream visions, day-dreams or night-dreams, as you would so-called real scenes, even allowing that the abstractions which move so dynamically when closed eye-lids are pressed are actually perceived. Become aware of the fact that you are not only influenced by the visual phenomenon which you are focused upon and attempt to sound the depths of all visual influence. There is no need for the mind's eye to be dead-ened after infancy, yet in these times the development of visual understanding is almost universally forsaken.

This is an age which has no symbol for death other than the skull and bones of one stage of decomposition...and it is an age which lives in fear of total annihilation. It is a time haunted by sexual sterility yet almost universally incapable of perceiving the phallic nature of every destructive manifestation of itself. It is an age which artificially seeks to project itself materialisti-cally into abstract space and to fulfill itself mechanically be-cause it has blinded itself to almost all external reality within eyesight and to the organic awareness of even the physical movement properties of its own perceptibility. The earliest cave paintings discovered demonstrate that primitive man had a greater understanding than we do that the object of fear must be objectified. The entire history of erotic magic is one of posses-sion of fear thru holding it. The ultimate searching visualiza-tion has been directed toward God out of the deepest possible human understanding that there can be no ultimate love where there is fear. Yet in this contemporary time how many of us even struggle to deeply perceive our own children?

The artist has carried the tradition of visual and visualiza-tion down through the ages. In the present time a very few have continued the process of visual perception in its deepest sense and transformed their inspirations into cinematic experiences. They create a new language made possible by the moving pic-ture image. They create where fear before them has created the greatest necessity. They are essentially preoccupied by and deal imagistically with—birth, sex, death, and the search for God.

the camera eye

Oh transparent hallucination, superimposition of image, mirage of movement, heroine of a thousand and one nights (Scheherazade must surely be the muse of this art), you obstruct the light, muddle the pure white beaded screen (it perspires) with your shuffling patterns. Only the spectators (the unbelievers who attend the carpeted temples where coffee and paintings are served) think your spirit is in the illuminated occasion (mistaking your sweaty, flaring, rectangular body for more than it is). The devout, who break popcorn together in your humblest double-feature services, know that you are still being born, search for your spirit in their dreams, and dare only dream when in contact with your electrical reflection. Unknowingly, as innocent, they await the priests of this new religion, those who can stir cinematic entrails divinely. They await the prophets who can cast (with the precision of Confucian sticks) the characters of this new order across filmic mud. Being innocent, they do not consciously know that this church too is corrupt; but they react with counter hallucinations, believing in the stars, and themselves among these Los Angelic orders. Of themselves, they will never recognize what they are awaiting. Their footsteps, the dumb drum which destroys cinema. They are having the dream piped into their homes, the destruction of the romance thru marriage, etc.

So the money vendors have been at it again. To the catacombs then, or rather plant this seed deeper in the undergrounds beyond false nourishing of sewage waters. Let it draw nourishment from hidden uprising springs channeled by gods. Let there be no cavernous congregations but only the network of individual channels, that narrowed vision which splits beams beyond rainbow and into the unknown dimensions. (To those who think this is waxing poetic, squint, give the visual objects at hand their freedom, and allow the distant to come to you; and when mountains are moving, you will find no fat in this prose.) Forget ideology, for film unborn as it is has no language and speaks like an aborigine—monotonous rhetoric. Abandon aesthetics—the moving picture image without religious foundations, let alone the cathedral, the art form, starts its search for God with only the danger of accepting an architectural inheritance from the categorized "seven," other arts its sins, and closing its circle, stylish circle, therefore zero. Negate technique, for film, like America, has not been discovered yet, and mechanization, in the deepest possible sense of the word, traps both beyond measuring even chances—chances are these twined searches may someday orbit about the same central negation. Let film be. It is something...becoming. (The above being for creator and spectator alike in searching, an ideal of anarchic religion where all are priests both giving and receiving, or rather witch doctors, or better witches, or...O, for the unnameable).

And here, somewhere, we have an eye (I'll speak for myself) capable of any imagining (the only reality). And there (right there) we have the camera eye (the limitation, the original liar); yet lyre sings to the mind so immediately (the exalted selectivity one wants to forget that its strings can so easily make puppetry of human motivation (for form as finality) dependent upon attunation, what it's turned to (ultimately death) or turned from (birth) or the way to get out of it (transformation). I'm not just speaking of that bird on fire (not thinking of circles) or of Spengler (spirals neither) or of any known progression (nor straight lines) logical formation (charted levels) or ideological formation (mapped for scenic points of interest); but I am speaking for possibilities (myself), infinite possibilities (preferring chaos).

And here, somewhere, we have an eye capable of any imaginings. And then we have the camera eye, its lenses grounded to achieve 19th-century Western compositional perspective (as best exemplified by the 19th-century architectural conglomeration of details of the "classic" ruin) in bending the light and limiting the frame of the image just so, its standard camera and projector speed for recording movement geared to the feeling of the ideal slow Viennese waltz, and even its tripod head, being the neck it swings on, balled with bearings to permit it that *Les Sylphides* motion (ideal to the contemplative romantic and virtually restricted to horizontal and vertical movements (pillars and horizon lines), a diagonal requiring a major adjustment, its lenses coated or provided with filters, its light meters balanced, and its color film manufactured, to produce that picture postcard effect (salon painting) exemplified by those oh so blue skies and peachy skins.

By deliberately spitting on the lens or wrecking its focal intention, one can achieve the early stages of impressionism. One can make this prima donna heavy in performance of image movement by speeding up the motor, or one can break up movement, in a way that approaches a more direct inspiration of contemporary human eye perceptibility of movement, by slowing the motion while recording the image. One may hand hold the camera and inherit worlds of space. One may over- and under-expose the film. One may use the filters of the world, fog, downpours, unbalanced lights, neons with neurotic color temperatures, glass which was never designed for a camera, or even glass which was but which can be used against specifications, or one may photograph an hour after sunrise or an hour before sunset, those marvelous taboo hours when the films labs will guarantee nothing, or one may go into the night with a specified daylight film or vice versa. One may become the supreme trickster, with hatfulls of all the rabbits listed above breeding madly. One may, out of incredible courage, become Méliès, that marvelous man who gave even the "art of the film" its beginning in magic. Yet Méliès was not witch, witch doctor, priest, or even sorcerer. He was a 19th-century stage magician. His films *are* rabbits.

What about the hat? or if you will, the stage, the page, the ink, the hieroglyphic itself, the pigment shaping that original drawing, the musical and/or all other instruments for copula-and-then-procreation? Kurt Sachs talks sex (which fits the hat neatly) in originating musical instruments, and Freud's revitalization of symbol charges all contemporary content in art. Yet possession thru visualization speaks for fear-of-death as motivating force—the tomb art of the Egyptian, etc. And then there's "In the beginning," "Once upon a time," or the very concept of a work of art being a "Creation." Religious motivation only reaches us thru the anthropologist these days—viz., Frazer on a golden bough. And so it goes—ring around the rosary, beating about the bush, describing. One thread runs clean thru the entire fabric of expression—the trick-and-effect. And between those two words, somewhere, magic...the brush of angel wings, even rabbits leaping heavenwards and, given some direction, language corresponding. Dante looks upon the face of God and Rilke is head among the angelic orders. Still the Night Watch was tricked by Rembrandt and Pollack was out to produce an effect. The original word was a trick, and so were all the rules of the game that followed in its wake. Whether the instrument be musical or otherwise, it's still a hat with more rabbits yet inside the head wearing it—i.e., thought's trick, etc. Even The Brains for whom thought's the world, and the word and visi-or-audibility of it, eventually end with a Ferris wheel of a solar system in the middle of the amusement park of the universe. They know it without experiencing it, screw it lovelessly, find "trick" or "effect" derogatory terminology, too close for comfort, are utterly unable to comprehend "magic." We are either experiencing (copulating) or conceiving (procreating) or very rarely both are balancing in that moment of living, loving, and creating, giving and receiving, which is so close to the imagined divine as to be more unmentionable than "magic."

In the event you didn't know "magic" is realmed in "the

imaginable," the moment of it being when that which is imagined dies, is penetrated by mind and known rather than believed in. Thus "reality" extends its picketing fence and each is encouraged to sharpen his wits. The artist is one who leaps that fence at night, scatters his seeds among the cabbages, hybrid seeds inspired by both the garden and wits-end forest where only fools and madmen wander, seeds needing several generations to be...finally proven edible. Until then they remain invisible, to those with both feet on the ground, yet prominent enough to be tripped over. Yes, those unsightly bulges between those oh so even rows will find their flowering moment...and then be farmed. Are you really thrilled at the sight of a critic tentatively munching artichokes? Wouldn't you rather throw overalls in the eventual collegic chowder? Realize the garden as you will — the growing is mostly underground. Whatever daily care you may give it—all is planted only by moonlight. However you remember it—everything in it originates elsewhere. As for the unquotable magic—it's as indescribable as the unbound woods it comes from.

(A foot-on-the-ground-note: The sketches of T. E. Lawrence's "realist" artist companion were scratches to Lawrence's Arab friends. Flaherty's motion picture projection of *Nanook of the North* was only a play of lights and silhouettes to the Aleutian Islander Nanook himself. The schizophrenic does see symmetrically, does believe in the reality of Rorschach, yet he will not yield to the suggestion that pinpoint light in a darkened room will move, being the only one capable of perceiving its stasis correctly. Question any child as to his drawing and he will defend the "reality" of what you claim to be "scribbles." Answer any child's question and he will shun whatever quest he'd been beginning.)

Light, lens concentrated, either burns negative film to a chemical crisp which, when lab washed, exhibits the blackened pattern of its ruin or, reversal film, scratches the emulsion to eventually bleed it white. Light, again lens concentrated, pierces white and casts its shadow-patterned self to reflect upon the spectator. When light strikes a color emulsion, multiple chemical layers restrict its various wave lengths, restrain its bruises to eventually produce a phenomenon unknown to dogs. Don't think of creatures of uncolored vision as restricted, but wonder, rather, and marvel at the known internal mirrors of the cat which catch each spark of light in the darkness and reflect it to an intensification. Speculate as to insect vision, such as the bee's sense of scent thru ultraviolet perceptibility. To search for human visual realities, man must, as in all other homo motivation, transcend the original physical restrictions and inherit worlds of eyes. The very narrow contemporary moving visual reality is exhausted. The belief in the sacredness of any man-achievement sets concrete about it, statutes becoming statues, needing both explosives and earthquakes for disruption. As to the permanency of the present or any established reality, consider in this light and thru most individual eyes that without either illumination or photographic lens, any ideal animal might claw the black off a strip of film or walk ink-footed across transparent celluloid and produce an effect for projection identical to a photographed image. As to color, the earliest color films were entirely hand painted a frame at a time. The "absolute realism" of the motion picture image is a human invention.

What reflects from the screen is shadow play. Look, there's no real rabbit. Those ears are index fingers and the nose a knuckle interfering with the light. If the eye were more perceptive it would see the sleight of 24 individual pictures and an equal number of utter blacknesses every second of the show. What incredible films might ultimately be made for such an eye. But the machine has already been fashioned to outwit even that perceptibility, a projector which flashes advertisement at subliminal speed to up the sale of popcorn. Oh, slow-eyed spectator, this machine is grinding you out of existence. Its electrical

storms are manufactured by pure white frames interrupting the
flow of the photographed images, its real tensions are a dynamic interplay of two-dimensional shapes and lines, the horizon line and background shapes battering the form of the
horseback rider as the camera moves with it, the curves of the
tunnel exploding away from the pursued, camera following, and
tunnel perspective converging on the pursuer, camera preceding,
the dream of the close-up kiss being due to the linear purity of
facial features after cluttersome background, the entire film's
soothing syrup being the depressant of imagistic repetition, a
feeling akin to counting sheep to sleep. Believe in it blindly, and
it will fool you — mind-wise, instead of sequins on cheesecloth
or max-manufactured make-up, you'll see stars. Believe in it eye-
wise, and the very comet of its overhead throw from projector to
screen will intrigue you so deeply that its fingering play will
move integrally with what's reflected, a comet-tail integrity
which would lead back finally to the film's creator. I am meaning, simply, that the rhythms of change in the beam of illumination which now goes entirely over the heads of the audience
would, in the work of art, contain in itself some quality of a
spiritual experience. As is, and at best, that hand spreading its
touch toward the screen taps a neurotic chaos comparable to the
doodles it produces for reflection. The "absolute realism" of
the motion picture image is a 20th-century, essentially Western,
illusion.

Nowhere in its mechanical process does the camera hold
either mirror or candle to nature. Consider its history. Being machine, it has always been manufacturer of the medium, mass-
producer of stilled abstract images, its virtue—related variance,
the result—movement. Essentially, it remains fabricator of a visual language, no less a linguist than the typewriter. Yet in the
beginning, each of an audience thought himself the camera,
attending a play or, toward the end of the purely camera career,
being run over by the unedited filmic image of a locomotive

which had once rushed straight at the lens, screaming when a revolver seemed fired straight out of the screen, motion of picture being the original magic of medium. Méliès is credited with the first splice. Since then, the strip of celluloid has increasingly revealed itself suited to transformations beyond those conditioned by the camera. Originally Méliès' trickery was dependent upon starting and stopping the photographic mechanism and between times creating, adding objects to its field of vision, transformations, substituting one object for another, and disappearances, removing the objectionable. Once the celluloid could be cut, the editing of filmic images began its development toward Eisensteinian montage, the principal of 1 plus 2 making 3 in moving imagery as anywhere else. Meantime labs came into the picture, playing with the illumination of original film, balancing color temperature, juggling double imagery in superimposition, adding all the acrobatic grammar of the film inspired by D.W. Griffith's dance, fades to mark the montage sentenced motion picture paragraph, dissolves to indicate lapse of time between interrelated subject matter, variations in the framing for the epic horizontal composition, origin of Cinemascope, and vertical picture delineating character, or the circle exclamating a pictorial detail, etc. The camera itself taken off the pedestal, began to move, threading its way in and around its source of material for the eventual intricately patterned fabric of the edited film. Yet editing is still in its 1, 2, 3 infancy, and the labs are essentially still just developing film, no less trapped by the standards they're bearing than the camera by its original mechanical determination. No very great effort has ever been made to interrelate these two or three processes, and already another is appearing possible, the projector as creative instrument with the film show a kind of performance, celluloid or tape merely source of material to the projectioning interpreter, this expression finding its origins in the color, or the scent, or even the musical organ, its most recent manifestations

— the increased programming potential of the IBM and other electronic machines now capable of inventing imagery from scratch. Considering then the camera eye as almost obsolete, it can at last be viewed objectively and, perhaps, view-pointed with subjective depth as never before. Its life is truly all before it. The future fabricating machine in performance will invent images as patterned after cliché vision as those of the camera, and its results will suffer a similar claim to "realism," IBM being no more God nor even a "Thinking machine" than the camera eye all-seeing or capable of creative selectivity, both essentially restricted to "yes-no," "stop-go," "on-off," and instrumentally dedicated to communication of the simplest sort. Yet increased human intervention and control renders any process more capable of balance between sub-and-objective expression, and between those two concepts, somewhere, soul... The second stage of transformation of image editing revealed the magic of movement. Even though each in the audience then proceeded to believe himself part of the screen reflection, taking two-dimension visual characters as his being within the drama, he could not become every celluloid sight running thru the projector, therefore allowance of another viewpoint, and no attempt to make him believe his eye to be where the camera eye once was has ever since proven successful—excepting the novelty of three-dimension, audiences jumping when rocks seemed to avalanche out of the screen and into the theater. Most still imagine, however, the camera a recording mechanism, a lunatic mirroring, now full of sound and fury presenting its half of a symmetrical pattern, a kaleidoscope with the original pieces of glass missing and their movement removed in time. And the instrument is still capable of winning Stanford's bet about horse-hooves never all leaving the ground in galloping, though Stanford significantly enough used a number of still cameras with strings across the track and thus inaugurated the flip-pic of the penny arcade, Hollywood still racing after the horse. Only when the fans move on to another track can the course be cleared for this eye to interpret the very ground, perhaps to discover its non-solidity, to create a contemporary Pegasus, without wings, to fly with its hooves, beyond any imagining, to become gallop, a creation. It can then inherit the freedom to agree or disagree with 2000 years of Western equine painting and attain some comparable aesthetic stature. As is, the "absolute realism" of the motion picture image is a contemporary mechanical myth. Consider this prodigy for its virtually untapped talents, viewpoints it possesses more readily recognizable as visually non-human yet within the realm of the humanly imaginable. I am speaking of its speed for receptivity which can slow the fastest motion for detailed study, or its ability to create a continuity for time compression, increasing the slowest motion to a comprehensibility. I am praising its cyclopean penetration of haze, its infra-red visual ability in darkness, its just developed 360-degree view, its prismatic revelation of rainbows, its zooming potential for exploding space and its telephonic compression of same to flatten perspective, its micro- and macroscopic revelations. I am marvelling at its Schlaeran self capable of representing heat waves and the most invisible air pressures, and appraising its other still camera developments which may grow into motion, its rendering visible the illumination of bodily heat, its transformation of ultra-violets to human cognizance, its penetrating x-ray. I am dreaming of the mystery camera capable of graphically representing the form of an object after it's been removed from the photographic scene, etc. The "absolute realism" of the motion picture is unrealized, therefore potential, magic.

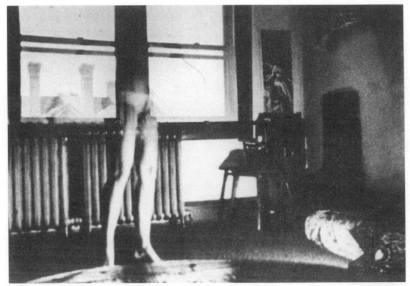

Sexual Meditation

my eye

My eye, turning toward the imaginary, will go to any wave-lengths for its sights. I'm writing of cognizance, mind's eye awareness of all addressing vibrations. What rays pass through this retina still unretained by mind? How long has sight's center continued pupil to other men's imaginings? This sensitive instrument must respond to all the gods who will deign to play upon it. Now as with the other four receptacles it too much fears The Devil, postulates "sights" as the end of its vibratory travels, remains bottled against any sinking, sticks to the surface to avoid ballooning into unfamiliar waves of unknown spaces, humanly preferring the certain breakers which will eventually shore it, scattering fragments, reflective surfaces and magnifiers of word here, and a moving picture there, of what was once an internal continuing composition. For the one sea, once seen, becomes a wavering weary-summation, dulls, palls receptivity to the distant surf hush, known Siren only when beyond all but a smashed salvation. Even the inside-out decomposes belief in the message heavenly destined for the sole comprehension of God-The-Beachcomber. Still, within these limitations, my eye begins a movement toward realms less imagined than the sands of heaven, risks more than ordinary flight, plots land escaping to a sub-terrain.

It all begins with the art, the necessity to create—for what? —that explanation changing time to Time, the young man dreaming of deification, not seeing himself as mere star—immortality rather casting his whole name in astral lights, spelled correctly for all time—beginning this pursuit patterned after others, in essentially non-religious era "The Lives of the Artists" becoming initiates' Bible, all ending as youth loses sense of growth for ever, scents his decay, and comes to know, for all the remembering of him, he will die. In that instant he either falls spiritually on the spot or begins to bend at the knees. In anger at his uneternalness, that he'll never see his biography unless his autos it himself, the aesthete begins cocooning toward his innards by demanding immediate return, release in creation, self-knowledge, etc. When each expression refuses echo and he discovers art unmirrors, this budding Narcissus either builds a boat, sits banked waiting for his reflection, or plunges in. From here on out all endeavor depends on depth, and all reasoning only confuses each issue. He exhausts excuses until each art work seems more sneeze than statement. His entire being becoming instrument for the expression of incomprehensible forces, he finds *these*, not *his*, expressions mold him after the fashion they will any attenuated audience. Being the medium, however, he's more familiar with the material than most, inherits worlds of words if poet, sounds if composer, etc., these gifts, given only when unasked after, exclude from the early epileptic "fall-out," the floater, and the reflective one. Yet all fall, the artist "in" and only surviving thru a formal resistance granting the illusion of bottomless descent.

My eye, then, inspiralling, frictioning style-wise, being instrument for striking sparks, is bequeathed visions at every illumination it's struck to create... Similar vistas being available to any viewer willing to release his eye for comparable movement. My eye so lost in space that fall feels ascensional, so style-beguiled as to know no "reality," sea running down-up hill, willy-nilly, waves not known by their phosphorescence but thru aesthetic reflection only...similar illuminations possible for any viewer capable of understanding his very vision as a metaphoric creation either directly inspired by nature or watered down by the cliché sights of others.

My eye then, sky-wards, relaxed, all cloudless, mind as non-reflective as possible, (where will I find the words to describe it), my wakeful awareness...non-blue, near gold of it, God in it, flakes of God-gold of it falling as if down from it into my eyes.

In non-chicken-littleness, my eye opening out to it, now hedging wording it, mind's eye narrowing down to it, destroying it. Imagine the headline: THE SKY ISN'T BLUE, discovered by —on—while—etc. Impossibility of all of it. I sky-hypnotized, my eye involved without view, seeing thru the so-called color of it, discovering light, now sighting it down to "flakes," "God-gold," "falling," "down." Metaphors—feathers, snow, reign, all golden. My best descriptive is still the negative—"non-blue." Best sense of it—"discovering light." Best sentence—"Impossibility of all of it." Still there's some possible, even historical, precedence for it, i.e., human, world-making, "reality" to it. There are some cultures whose extensive scribblings never refer to the sky as blue, some who refer rather purely in terms of light. Look it up, if you will; or, better, look up to it, see for yourself. (In its deepest sense that would mean, forget all I've written here.) Additional note for parents or teachers: Please don't force your militantly Prussian or goblin Cobalt or any kind of crayon bluing into the drawings of yellow sky happy children, respect those young ones who use any and all of the wax spectrum, and marvel at those who remain still representationally dissatisfied.

Closing these eyelids, shutting Pandora's trap for awhile, believing even in the reality of it, thwarting thought awhile, traveling thru the blue sub-terrain?—marine?—what? seeming tunnels of it, (utterly unable to photograph any of it), purposeless in my wanderings around, seeming to be spiraling at times, timelessly, encountering shapes (indescribable), passing thru them, or were they passing thru me? or was a corner somewhere turned? into an unrepresented dimension, sometime, in this non-time, even the human drama projecting into these spaces, as if here too there were curtains to rise and fall, entrances, exits, and feeling of interrelation, some of these as-if shapes as if to be avoided, some of these imaginary colors unimaginable, alien even to this alien land-sea-what scape. I remember a once-upon-a-time shut-eye (but not sleep) adventure when I absolutely knew a certain very convex-or-concave hypothetically approaching, with marine-like motion, shape must not overcome me, i.e., envelope the entire field of eyelid vision, and my finally opening my eyes in an almost sexual sweat, wondering for hours how the drama had continued without me, whether eye-opening had excluded me, etc. There is a definite intent to manipulate these, mind's eye?, patterns and without hand in it or bodily weight, freedom from the physical world?, to influence this internal?, destiny as one humanly imagines any control, among infinite possibilities?, and a definite retention of imagistic, external?, superimpositions once eye's opened to the feeling of having cheated, having broken some original law?, in the act of opening eye. Thus the desire to rationalize the eyelid into a simple projection screen of one's own thought-provoked but rather irresponsible doodles...a thought having nothing to do with these sensory experiences other than the mind manipulating to escape them,—the realization of them, the eye open escape, being too difficult without physical paraphernalia (lacking camera, etc.)—the illusion of complete avoidance, unconsciousness, sleep, etc., preferable to the brain. Yet that instrument, in some perverse moment, grants retention of the retinal eye's adventure and this inadequate description of the experience, perhaps the first civilized touch upon this optical territory, the first move meant to eventually colonize. Otherwise that chaos too would have to be humanly avoided. After all, the mind minds. The only way to know these visions as a world not just thought up is to experience them as a world to be thought about which will eventually make of them a round world thought full, description, which is to know them only as a world thought down, narrowed, in the process of the brain's eternal creation or dead recreation, as you will. Here is a realm waiting better than Columbuses to discover it, demanding greater flights than rockets, existing in its own right. My wife, thru the needling eye of extreme concentration, has been able to retain the fabric of shut eye patterns with her lids wide open and thread her sight thru both sensory worlds at once, moving toward the sense of their interrelatedness. I am not seamstress enough for the experience yet, lacking patience, wanting to force, tear even veils without recognizable substance, either raping or retreating in a sexual sweat. My wife waits, receives, inspires my vision, as always, yet receives her source of inspiration in my art—seen as a closed widening circle only superficially, as widening ripple O's on the surface of water not perceived depth-wise—the art, each work, as past—cast—a completely other world—in a space of its own—known because given thru human motivation—the impetus of its space-time existence—incomparably inspirational—disturbing air-H²O-soil-all world otherwise known—according to depth of perception—dependent on where and how far the eye will follow All the above and all below, available to all.

My eye, again, outwards (without words) dealing with these "indescribable," "imaginary" vibrations, producing the categorized colors, best known negatively, this sensibility dealing with this phenomenon, an irresponsible gamble thwarting the trained response link between retina and brain, breaking the associational chain, this mind-eye partnership playing the game with an unmarked deck, as in the beginning, giving eye's mind a chance for a change, yet a deck all the same, only ship-shape for exploration, not a-bottled-trophy. (Drawing a string of language grown as impossibly rigid as contemporary bridge cards in comparison to their Tarot ancestors, I deck my prose with whatever puns come my way, aiming at deliberate ambiguity, hoping thereby to create a disbelief in the rigidity of any linguistic statement, knowing only poetry immortal enough to escape the rigorous belief in any one word-world as a sense-killing finality.) My eye, again, then, beginning its non-color, life-giving, continually created coursing, follows rainbows, no thought of a pot of gold allowed the mind, pursuing light, seeking to stare straight into the sun, yet humbly shunning no reflections, searching even electrical filaments, all fires. A bent black tube, toy spectroscope, broke up a light beam to shelve the colors in very neat rows for formal introduction, as lacking-daisical and hypocritical as histories on tombstones; still I began to differentiate in the shuffling of shelves, spectrum change, from light source to light source, came to know at least each mask, sun's mask, neon's mask, etc. Then began the identification of light source through the guise of reflection, sun's rays grass costumed, house bulb by way of rug, etc. Finally came the discovery of what costume added to the light source character, the subtlety of the shelving in the merging of "color" spanch to "other-color" spanch within the bent tubing, and cognizance of the vibrations between and within those, once thought of as dominant "color" solids, in discovering the moon's transformation of sun's rays, the "brown" varnished furniture's enchantment of fire source light, etc. The spectroscope itself then shelved, except for occasional reference in the contemporary game of also-being-somewhat-scientific which I am fortunately only childishly prey to, and the eye's flight discovery of its internal ability to produce prismatic sensations directly, without extraneous instruments. The original influence on this added venture was the prism, quickly discarded in the game and replaced by squint, allowance for the eyelashes to diffract the illumination prismatically. Finally, eyes wide open, the ray-like structure of the path of light, obviously still too influenced by Western sense of perspective, finding one vanishing point among bulb's filaments or at sun's center and radiating horizontally to the four corners of twin-trained eyes, and vertically to shatter among the lashes, contains within its web indescribable rainbows, still too influenced by the spectroscope and the prism, being imitative of each in arrangement of colors—"red-yellow-green-blue-purple"—yet exhibiting color oddities when the eye has been uninfluenced by scopism for a period of time. Under extreme non-concentration, fixed by effortless fascination, akin to self-hypnosis, my eye is able to retain for cognizance even those utterly unbanded rainbows reflecting off the darkest of objects, so transitory as to be completely unstructionable, yet retaining some semblance in arrangement to the source of illumination, bearing incredible resemblances to eyelid vision, pattering their tonal dance to the harmonics of all closed vi sion, yet differing in just that spectroscope arrangement. I am stating my given ability, prize of all above pursuing, to transform the light sculptured shapes of an almost dark-blackened room to the rainbow hued patterns of light without any scientific paraphernalia. I am even enabled to impose arbitrary selection upon this newly discovered sense ability, to choose one color toning, eye only filtering out all others, and perceive all light, either source or reflection, according to inclination...this cast of eye-dye finding its parallel in everyday ordinary vision due to lack of perception rather than selectivity — i.e., the seeing of a snow scene at twilight as essentially black and white or black and blue-white to the exclusion of all other coloration. I am finding now that all my seemingly speculative color pursuits have had precedence in my filmic statements, subconscious invitations which unfortunately needed the conscious approval, my low level taking more cognizance of the gadget, the science toy, than of my own aesthetic visionary encouragement. As eyes become freed of their introductory influences, they become increasingly subject to the inspiration of the art. Many will see this only as intro-spectrum. I say all is.

Within the immediately distinguishable—the "known" unseen. Without confusion—the vision fissures and dead. A way out—disconnection of tele-antenna for incoming calls. A way out of the distinct—out of focus...of soft focus...for the seen unknown—taken in, as an intake easy as breath, yet not absorbed...eye needing sense of irritation for its aliveness as well as any-living-thing else. In visual indistinction as other than ordinary outline emerges—to be effortlessly received. Without deliberation, an aura of sensual annoyance establishes itself. To round out all—this is the boundary of new visual phenomenon requiring alive perceptability. Forms merge, as the fingertips closing to touch, closely viewed, reach a blur of their color, changing their contour, visually merging with each other before physical contact; as all unattended forms in an emergency form formlessness, a something more or less than background; as all before faint. Within this aura of non-shape, shapes reshape, and as long as the eye breathes them naturally, sponse and response equally unconscious, they continue their transformatory dance until one is involved purely with the innards of what one once knew only as outline. Once cartoon sight has been utterly re-moved, the internal movement of each once-object subjectively reveals itself—an effervescence, an as-if bubbling up-out for viewability of spaceless timeless entities. Once my wife, reading Lady Murasaki's *Tales of Genji* aloud to me, began such a trans-formation while my attention was fixed to transcribing 20th-century Western prose into ancient Japanese imagery, my eyes being freed and abstractly receiving the reader, at first almost lip reading to take it all in, and then liberated thru extreme mental reconstructioning of word-sound to picture, all sight without thought, in indifference to differentiation, loosing visual solid-ity to an imagistic melt and then to something which should have been indescribable. But I received the experience "wisely," not being taken enough unawares, forgot Genji and warily thought my way thru the experience, calling on mind to supply metaphoric explanations, recognizing a continual evolution by stages—rather than otherwise having the sense of the adventure, being attenuated to the external call and allowing only most dis-tant internal echo, leaving ego's platform out of it. But because I missed, used, the experience, I am better enhaloed by what had been back-lighting, and the ring of it eventually spread to contour what had been the outline of her hair, then suffused the natural brownish color until white, her facial changes keeping pace with this aging process until every shadowed area had cracked across her features into wavering wrinkles eventually isolating the paler manifestations to the impermanent shape of a skull. Fear constricted me to glances then, and each sharpening of vision forced the imagery back to what I'd recognize as "normal." Yet reassured by my sense-destructive abilities, and all curiousity aroused, I stopped short of normalcy, with my wife's still-white hair now streaming down beyond any brown length of it, pooling at her feet, and enclosing what was once her form entirely, I allowed the process to undevelop again, "undevelop" occurring to the mind as it remembers the second, lesser, evolution more negatively than the original, hair being almost the reverse of its ordinary manifestation and shadows this time shaping a skull while whitened areas palled to a variety of unrecognizable, yet continually akin to my wife's, features. As features became unbelievably aged, they constricted into a more believable infant aspect, hair aura suffusing throughout the room. My mental insistence on the drama gave me the sense that dead and unborn relatives were presenting themselves thru the living organism, my wife suddenly a spaceless entity containing a timeless evolution. This thought, a devastating limitation upon happenstance, constricted all reception and stopped the process dead. Later times my wife and I have both sought to artificially recreate the experience for study. Restricted as we were to other considerations, "times," "art," "study," etc., we could adventure no further than to surround each other with a promissory aura which never developed internally. Undevelopment is what's needed, from positive, thru negative to some unexposed original. Those non-times when the happening imposed itself successfully upon us are indescribable and altogether too personally sacred for even a literary attempt, my true expression being the visual medium of film. Only one of these later occurrences was unsuccessful enough to bear transcription. In anger, coupled with a frustration at my inability to even attempt to communicate with my wife, I saw her head reshape itself through the emergence of animal forces, most particularly and recurrently the head of a dog, an animal she has always felt related to. My wife describes this same scene, her seeing of me in that silence and thru her limiting anger, as if seen thru heat waves which distorted my form in terms of size more than change of shape, my becoming larger than ordinarily perceived, my concentrated visage, or rather something simply referred to as "you," filling my wife's field of vision, then diminishing to a size more normal yet presenting an aspect abnormally wavering as if inbounded and again able to assume giant proportions. Technical description: "I was watching a movie photographed thru a zoom lens and rippled glass." This episode ended when the source of illumination, a bulb, blew out, leaving us both with an unmistakable electrical burnt scent in the air.

There is then an akin-to-the-soft-focus-vision accomplished thru exactly opposite procedures, relative to hyper-focal clarity, and dependent on spatial indefiniteness. Self-hypnosis here is approximated thru a fixity, rather than laxity, of gaze. Willful attention, forced beyond the natural capacity for mental absorption, produces a willy-nilliness less memory-dominated than when one is unegoed. Here one seems more practitioner than patient, and patience is not as necessary. One feels less hypnotic and more as if hypnotiser of the object, "objectivity" a descriptive of this process. All optic nerves must remain strained, beyond any ordinary attentive sighting, until they are as truly, tho oppositely, involved with "the linear" as one is when focally negating alignment. The nerve ends must be as if drawn out to see all objects as if penciled. They must become identified with "the line" beyond any delineation. "Space" is what must cease to exist. The rationality which will be activated by these procedures must be turned to the destruction of all two- or three-dimensional logic. One may, for instance, feed the mind with the fact that in contemporary mathematics many problems are "solved" by allowing the problematical existence of many more dimensions than the realist, essentially Western Renaissance, three. Or one may simply allow the brain to wander among the multiple vanishing points and horizon lines of many Renaissance masterpieces and exhaust mental restrictions within those labyrinthian expressions. One cannot here diminish-vert-or-stract the intellect but must maintain a sense originating argument with all its restrictive manifestations. Thus concentrated once upon my wife's arm, elbow to hand, my eyes drew every possible line out of it until all seemed strands separated as if in a dissection of its light and shadow surface. Then a semi-reformation produced multiple arms, moving independently in this re-defined space, superimposing over each other, all differently drawn. The shaded area of the knuckles, the inbetween finger cast shadows, the very hair of the arm and the crackling blackened wrinkles produced a number of finely-drawn caricatures afloat without apparent interdependence. Eventually it became impossible for me to discern the originating image. At this point my mind, seeking to re-define "reality," wondered if my own hand so split-up would have a complementary image of itself for reaching out to touch or otherwise sense, to grasp or otherwise move in interrelationship, with each of my wife's imagistic offspring; and it then postulated an attempt to connect parent hands to this intent. The instant the singular image of my blundering fingers began to pry into this multiple exposure—the vision vanished, all lines snaking to their source. As in all previous examples of supernatural vision, my wife and I have both experienced a number of more successful eye adventures in this respect which are completely beyond any linguistic expression whatsoever.

If one were to turn an adventuring eye to literary correspondence, facsimilating visual adventure with similarly adventuring literature, transforming optic abstract impressions into non-representational language, enchanting non-sights into non-words, one could write only sound poems, the audio manifestation of letters not being restricted to a pre-determined logic and rather communicating on an emotional level only distantly related to all known word origins of any written sound. Withing that distant relationship is the embryonic form of a purely onomatopoeic art. The visual parallel of this art is being created by men already termed "abstract expressionist," who are fashioning the symbol-cuneiform-hieroglyphic-letters for future communication. The moving picture enables the development of continuity and therefore an evolution upon language as we contemporarily know it. All contained within this book has died in the womb. I abort it to save the living organism, its origins…itself a specimen…at least a museum piece…of value only to the anatomical eye.

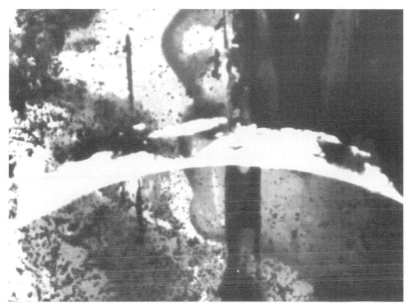

Dog Star Man

his story

, , , BEING ENTIRELY COMPOSED OF SCRIPT AND
SCERIARIO FRAGMENTS SO LITER-REALIZED THAT THE NECESSITY
TO VISUALIZE THEM NEVER COMPULSIONED THE FILMING OF THEM.

(This *Of Ocean*, San Francisco, 1953)
The flow of black waves inward, smoothly building up them-
    selves, forming a semi-diagonal line as the camera pans with
    them.
The flow of this line, faster now and forming more of a vertical
    pattern than a diagonal one.
With quickened tempo the line of mounting water moves to-
    ward a vertical pattern as the white crusts of toppling waves
    begin to appear.
The whitened tops of the waves suddenly reach the zenith of
    their vertical composition. The contrasting horizontal of the
    waves head on approaching and...
Exploding horizontally against black rocks in the foreground...
    Exploding horizontally larger with the rocks formlng only a
    thin ridge at the bottom...
And exploding in all directions with no visible rocks but only a
    burst of water filling the frame.

(Untitled script fragment, Central City, Colo., 1953)
A moon uncentered, round and white as ice.
A sun scratched mud pool. The revealing of fingers of snow
    which feed it. Then the pure white of their source.
Night and the uncentered moon overcome by clouds.
A street-lit passageway of stairs leading nowhere.
Stars.
House lights patterning a mountainside with squares on black.
Fast movement over snow to a child's hand scooping a white ball.

The alive face of a child.

The sun.

The slow movement of the snowball breaking the mud pool into
its components.

The hand of the child flowering open against the sky.

The laughing face and eyes of the child and a movement of
laughter across town houses blurred across valley to the daylit
mountain side.

Victorian filigree pointing icily down to the crow-lined face of
the mother calling across a wash of valley to the road where a
child stops play.

Disappointment in child's clothes, from capped face down to
awkward toes and a frozen mud hole in the earth.

The fingers of the child close.

Lines of water straight as arrows rush together to their foam.

The white stream of a woman's back to the dark of her hair
her hand arranging.

Rocks foam-etched in water rush.

Fingers tenderly out of hand into hair.

A pool of the stream forever circling within itself.

Mirror white with the face of the woman appearing.

The dream of her eyes drifting—all the white of her face in
motion.

A shift of snow scene with two dogs racing play.

Their leaps to sky.

Their curves on white.

The poise of one.

The flash of the other.

Teeth meeting.

Angry fur.

Flowers of blood petal the snow.

Coals glow into flights of fire.

The leap of the flesh of a man's face in the play of light and dark.

Ribbons of snow lie on the mountain slopes.

Clouds reach for the sun.

The dark mud pools glisten and beyond them, up a dirt road, a man walks head down oblivious of the mountain town passing behind him.

A church tower large in its symbology hovers over the roofs of the town down to the dirt road and the solitary figure of the man moving speck-like against black mud bands through snow.

The sharp dark profile of his head as he looks up to the mountainside dominated by the white of the church with the partially clouded sun behind its tower.

His face uplifted to wag in the direction of the church, the road passing in wrinkled ruts beneath him until he steps suddenly into its mud pools with a splash.

The explosion of water up all around him as he whirls furiously to regain his balance.

The contorted lines of his face as he curses. Drawing back he looms against the blank of the sky.

The beauty of worlds of bubbles in motion.

The circles of water widening out.

The curved lines of water straightening into parallels in movement.

The rippled sun growing round in the calm of the waters.

The curved lines in the white of snow hills.

The shadow lines of mountains whitened.

The stretches of curves and whorls to white horizon lines where the sun is setting.

(Unfinished. *Dog Star Man*, Denver, 1954)

A moon uncentered, round and white as ice.

Beneath it pine trees spread their wings in wind against the snow. They pass again to darkness.

House lights pattern a mountainside with squares on black.

One window holds a Mother where she rocks and the white cottoned form of a girl Child armed in sleep. They weave dreamily through curtaining.

The Mother smiles through lace.

Her hand strokes the Child beyond strings of patterning.

Pattern mists the Child's face in a sketeh of dream white.

Cotton wrinkles shift across cotton body Child.

The Mother whiles time away rocking, clothes her eyes in perfect peace.

The moon as down is struggling in the hands of clouds.

The Mother is aware, as arrested as animal, of the night without.

The child face shifts on awakening's edge. Her mouth yawns a silent scream in sleep.

The window is square with black, and the mother rises within its frame. She looms large through the threads of the curtains, moves heavily with her burden, then draws the shade line strong down.

Down night to the points of arched windows whose lit oblongs contain the shadow form of a Young Man.

His other side is warmed by a living room, his form still etched to the flowered walls of the room edge him in, then his Mother knitting precisely on the one side, his Father shifting newspapers on the other

Young Man turns to stare the length of the room.

The room in reverse. Young Man's Mother and Father are in position at the far end of it

They follow Young Man's movement out of the room with their eyes.

Out the window and up to where its points dance as flames kindled to the distant glass above lighting against the dark of the house.

The face of the Young Man as candle dances softly beside a clock.

Young Man stoops to something unseen. The clock moves by and the room turns to a world of patchwork quilt.

The kingdom of quilt gives way to Young Man's hand. The bed is white as blank.

The face of the Young Man ghostlit beside the pure tower of the
    candle.
Pine angels fade in and out of the night.
The candle flickers to a tiny point. Lines of fingers rush to
    guard it.

(Finished *Dog Star Night*, Central City, 1955)
The night lighted squares of the windows of houses irregularly
    scattered up the side of a mountain. The shadow form of a
    man moves up and blots out one by one each nest of win-
    dows until all is black.
Titles: white on black.
The night street of an ancient mountain town, alive with the
    electricity of saloon signs and plate glass fronts, moving
    placidly where three hunters drink and two people, a man and
    a women, sit in the foreground at a table. Suddenly, the quick
    turned face of the young woman in surprise and fright.
The moon crossed by clouds.
The face of a man is seen as a negative through the plate glass
    staring in with fixed eyes. He is distorted in anger.
The flash of bulbs illuminating a saloon sign outside.
The window in positive, empty of anyone.
The fingers of the woman creeping tremblingly up over her own
    face more wondering than frightened.
A young man sitting with her at the table stuporing over his
    drink. He looks up at her with suddenly ogling eyes.
His wobbling view of her as she tries to smile.
The bar and those lined up alongside it—the first hunter stand-
    ing beside his gun turns slowly toward her.
Wobbling view across the young man, across the table, finally rest-
    ing on the woman looking quickly questioningly in his direction.
The second hunter sitting at the bar sliding off his stool to stare
    across the room in her direction.
Wobbling view up to the face of the woman.

The third hunter turning quickly in her direction.

Hesitating view wobbling between his two companions and finally resting on the woman.

The three hunters staring in the direction of the woman, each drunkenly stepping, watching steadfixedly.

The view moving in on the woman.

The view inching out all else around her

The view wobbling in close on her face broken with sweat.

The hand of the young man reaching aross the table to her hand fingering itself away to hide beneath the table.

The eyes of the woman in negative and rolling frantically in their sockets.

The ground blurring by underfoot.

Shadows fuming across the face of the woman turning.

Shadows flicking across the face of the man at the window. He turns in her direction.

The man and the woman on horseback and in slowed motion riding. Their ups and downs are those of a merry-go-round.

The woman leaning back into the sky with arms thrown widely.

The man riding low on the neck of his steed.

The woman thrown back.

The woman falling, slowly grounded.

The man tumbling forward down.

The sun whirling through the black branches of trees.

The fingers of the woman scratching earth.

The sun through trees.

Her fingers gripping.

The sun through trees.

His hands moving under the cloth of her shirt.

His other hand moving under her thigh.

The blinding sun uncaught and clear.

Her hands as fists.

The face of the woman struggling up away from him.

Her hands like birds whipping his face.

Her face breaking into a scream which carries across trees,
across sun, across clear sky to three men standing on a knoll
by the two horses. Their guns move like scales in their hands.

The rifle of the first hunter rhythms time and then is suddenly
caught up to the firing position and the face of the hunter.

The face of the man now fixed in fright, down the checks of his
shirt in an even row down to his feet moving slowly backward.

The squinting eyes of the hunter and away from them along the
level of the gun.

The figure of the man turning to run.

The dance of his feet in the turn.

The checks of his shirt in a whirl.

The mouths of the other two hunters opening...

Along the level of the rifle to the mouth of the gun tearing a
hole of whiteness.

The trees circling...an upraised bloody hand countering their
movement.

The dead face of the man pivoting.

The counter motion of the trees.

The face of the woman opening into a slowed motion scream.

The trees down to the ground to blackness.

The eyes of the girl following down and down.

The negative eyes of the girl wild with memory.

The young man in the bar leaning sympathetically in her direction.

The door of the bar blown wide open.

The woman seen through the moving rungs of chairs.

The lighted doorway from outside the bar, the woman rushing
into its brilliance and then turning shadow as she steps into
the night.

A spot of blood flowering on the ground, then a trail of them.

The shadow of the man moving over the earth.

Three shadow forms struggling in the saloon doorway. The
young man is pulled back into the light by two of the hunters

and the door is closed.

The shadow of the man waiting across an expanse of broken rock. The shadow of the woman drifts in, hesitates, then joins the man shadow, crosses, turns, crosses, again.

The face of the woman as she circles the form of the man — the lights of the town whirl by behind her.

The clouds toying with the moon.

The shadow hands of the woman gliding along the ground.

The shadow hands of the man playing across the rocks.

The lighted squares of the town whirling.

The still of the moon.

The shadow fingers of the woman reaching out.

The white hand of her opening as a flower.

The shadow hand of the man stilled upon the earth.

The woman lowering to her knees and reaching downward.

The white hand of the woman tenderly resting at the edge of the shadow hand, fingering its shadow tips, then lifting dust out of the palm of its darkness.

The face of the woman lifting with her hand outstretched before her until her supplicating gesture looses the dust from between her fingers—it sifts down misting her features.

The shadow of the man interrupting the moon.

The woman abandoning herself beautifully to the earth. The shadow of the man crosses her body.

The moon as freed.

The moon shade of the man slowly blanketing her face...her eyes closing.

The rising of the moon.

The rising and turning of her white breast.

The lacing of the hands of man and woman.

The pure, pale curve of the woman's thigh—the intrusion of the haired knee of the man.

His arm circling the white of her back.

Her fingers playing upon the knolls of his vertebrae.

Their faces meeting and closing to a line between two forms of
white.
The pulsing line between the white of their two bodies.
The rivers of their twined legs.
The darker curves of their bodies turning into night
The hand of the woman as a star against the dark of the man's
hair.
The moon overcome by clouds again.
The hand of the woman fallen upon her moving breast sud-
denly stilled to a frozen pool of white star crossed.
The sun, fierce in a blank sky.
The crooked fingers of the woman hooked to her breast in this
new light.
The feet of the woman black against the ground.
Her other hand lost and cut among rocks.
Her face dead as her eyes are wide, her smile idiotic as the con-
tinual peace it suggests. And yet she is hauntingly beautiful.
Up to the forms of the hunters against the blasting sky. They
wag their heads.
The sun again and down to rope, down rope to the agonized face
of the man hanging by the neck, down his back to the sheriff
and his deputy standing beyond the hung form shaking their
heads.
The hand of the sheriff crossing his star to pull a knife from his
jacket pocket. Following his reaching up reveals the sign attached to the blood-ribboned front of the hanged man. It
reads "BEWARE THE DOG." Then the form of the man drops
down and all that is left is the blank of the sky.
THE END titles—black on white.

(Prose script, Denver, 1956)
Dissolves of mountains make great softnesses of them, a
mountain range becoming transitional as clouds. The low-
lands are a shift of scenes pin-pointing around twin lovers

against the grass. The dreams of geographic lines fade to the solidarity of their bodies. In the break the sun is the vision of the boy in a white blindness.

Each part of the girl's body then becomes a dream, dissolving into each other part, herself apart and each part transitory as the world he's thought to have inherited.

His lips move love-like.

Flickering shapes of mountains, sharp as lightning streaks.

Her eyes shift over terrain that catches like a net and holds fast to this clearing where life lines of flowering weeds stalk too close for comfort.

A hand crawls in the grass, its spider fingers searching out a prey. She stands and the horizon sinks around her. There is a house behind her, and a dark mountain, furred with trees.

Her hands fly to his clothes and she clutches him desperately, seemingly gathering him up into her arms. They kiss and the yarns of their body lines thread together. The valley and the mountain ranges spin around them. Something with five fingers creeps over a stone.

They run hand-linked together. And as they run their shadows lengthen before them and the shadows of the valley reach beyond them and the house itself is then in shadows and its windows flash lightning. It seems to take them until night to reach their destination. The landscape behind them, they race in as shadows into the shadows, enlargingly closer. They are laughing playfully, then breathlessly, then hysterically. And the door shuts black against the mountainous background, enclosing them in a dark hall with mirrors where they can see themselves and large stuffed animals on the walls. There is only the sound of their breathing.

The boy observes the animal heads, the serenity in a semblance of life, the glass blank of their stare. He is reflected in their eyes.

She stands uncertainly in the hallway. It is empty, yet there is a sense that something has passed through. The eyes of the animal heads are alive with a mysterious light, an electricity. She turns to the nearest mirror and sees a monstrous boy with a sense of such mysterious power yet beautiful calm that one would think of the walking dead, a trespasser from that world which guides all our lives with its strength yet remains detached in our memories. He is covered with blood and stands with an axe in hand. She turns as if to confront him, confronting only another mirror with his image still reflected, standing. She turns again in a rage and finds herself in her lover's arms.

The eyes of the animals die into the darks of their bodies.

. . . .

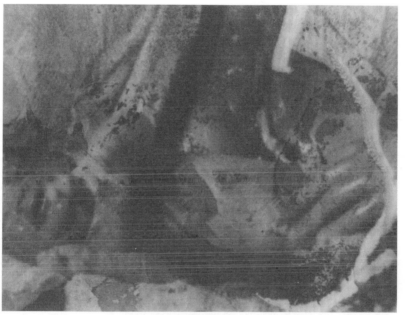

Thigh Line Lyre Triangular

notes of anticipaton

A continuation of "His Story." This, though, unrealized in words—hence the film, *Anticipation of the Night.*

The sun is a red ball in zig zags. It is a star which, alone, is without definitive course.

Only the mountainous horizon passing toward, beneath, and away from the sun fixes its movement into a line. The horizon passes above the sun as well as below.

The whirls of the sun splash into green leaves.

The earth curvatures, a continuity, fix its line—the sideways sweep of mountain hold its course.

The frantic rush of sun explodes on water in reflection.

The modulations of earthen movement converge from all sides upon the centered, stopped circle of the sun.

The whitening exposure of the sun as a rush forward blots against the shadow side of leaves.

The negative of the sun, as a bruise, whitens in gathering itself into the smallest circle.

Water becomes a whirlpool.

The horizoned mountains show their rocks.

The sun as cut bleeds across the horizon.

Its memory is the black negative of fire covering the earth, burning in the shadow trees, exploding against rushes of water.

The flowers trail a smoke which sinks.

The grasses are buried in gaseous streams of white.

A child's hand falls amongst fallen leaves.

Lovers' lips seek resting places in shadowed folds of flesh.

The light dies in an aged eye.

Two young men fight with glistening knives in the moonlight.

The rectangular squares of lights in houses shift.

SEQUENCE ORDER FOR SHOOTING *Night Film*

The rose as it may pertain to self.

The self reflective among tree shadows.

The self as a force of water.

The dance of the twilight children.

The children's faces in the night backed by artificial lighting.

The water spots as fallen stars.

The self reflected in black pools.

The fires of night.

The self afire.

The passage of night events, shifts of scene, explosions.

The self in a perpetual turn.

The drunkenness becoming sensual night.

The self as God.

The passages of memory as blocks of light suddenly thrown open.

The self in parts played out as on a stage.

The avalanches of white sheets.

Night Film

Twilight begins enclosed in the house with slants of sunlight picking out those symbols of the self which will play themselves out during the night.

The light play ends on the rose: reflected in black and shadowed on the wall.

The fire of light beneath its bowl.

The shadow play cast of leaf and water fire.

The rose itself—a color—then a fire.

The slant light as gold on lawn and tips of leaves.

The shadow of trees.

The rose at sunset.

The light

The water

The rose in water
The fire in water

The rose at sunset
The light
The shadow
The water
The rose in water
The light in water
The shadow in water
The fire

Sky with water (w & w)
Green gold white
Sky with water
Green gold white
White   White
Reveal rainbow   (promise of rainbow
White white   burning bush gold
Rainbow move   purple always in white)
White white
CU Rainbow move
Rainbow sequence
     (all white)
        then...
Burning bush
Rainbow into darks
    (sequence)
Green to gold fare
Gold to black
Green to gold fare
Gold to black
Green to gold fare to grass (alas)
Grass to dark

Dark to rose
Rose to pattern
to Dark
Dark to white
to dark
Dark to rose
Water & Rose
Dark to green
Grass — Child!

The Development of the Child
Pure white
Make hand on grass evolve out of
White struggle
Then green evolve to arm and into
White struggle
Make legs evolve out of white struggle
Then green evolve to legs and into
white struggle
Then white struggle evolve into

Bold to body arm to arm to green
        dark   to   light   to   dark

Body to hand to green
        dark   to light

Arm   to   body   to   body   body
light to dark to light to dark to light to dark

Structure of Amusementation
(From blur of lights (into cubes)
        (to freeze within which
   3
        (blur of children

Repeat 3

2   (blur of children
         (to freeze of child

Repeat 2

         (Freeze of child with blur
1   (of lights behind
         (To white of child in opposition

Repeat 1

         Variations—
Large flash away to large light
(white) in confusion to dark
Reappearance of distant moon traversed (or) to dis[*solve*]
lights in confusion
flash to appearance to dis moon
lights in confusion to red
Red to moon and dis
Moon move
Greens to light
light flashes
Greens, greens
Temple greens
Greens, greens to bars
Temple
Bars to light to greens

(insert dark scenes in dark trees)
flare to yellow-white
flare to trees to dark
(light flares to polar bears to dark
(dark to pink
         repeat
(dark to pink to boy
         repeat

(dark to pink to boy to flesh
      repeat
dark to pink to boy to flesh
flesh to face to girl & pillow
polar bears white to
pan girl to under pillow
scene
(repeat)
pan girl to under pillow
scene—neck join   theme and variations
(repeat)
trees in complexity jumps)
jump to rope)   )
trees to white   )
Shadow man   )

Best lift superfluous child pan to
find bird flight mix
Make greens consonant until reds are firmly established
Then mix pink PJ's to boy
Bird into red jungle under pillow
Then bird lingers to make flight
Then mating
All mix yellow and pink with blue
Boy pink take over
Through sheets to polar bear

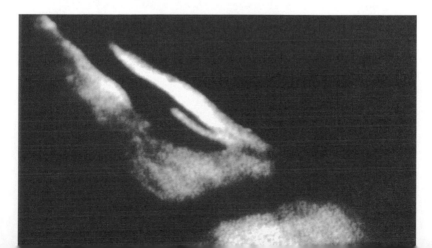

The trees to night

Out of darkness, the trees to trees movement ↖↗ showing very little contrasting blue and rose skies to darkness

Out of gold, the trees to clear skies (contrasting blue and reds) then to trees then to plains with trees then to trees and gold

Out of white, thru gold, to plains piling up with contrasting blues and reds to darkness, then reflections to the skies white, blues, reds to darkness, then trees, ~~white~~ ~~then~~ blues and reds, to darknesses to gold

    Gold to dark to gold

Shadow out ← to white
White bark to green
~~white to green to~~
Gold to green to white →
white to green to gold ←
White with rainbow ⊙ circular to green
Green to gold ~~streak~~ ←
Black with white ~~streak~~ →←
Green to gold ~~streak~~ ←
Black with white figurine
Green to gold ~~streak~~
Black with white ~~streak~~ + figurine
Shadow to green to gold to white (foreward)
~~Shadow~~ Green to gold to black with lights
The same
The ~~same~~
Black to white

Birth

The rose to pink
The skin to dark
The dark to rose to ~~or~~ green
The green to skin
The pink to green to pink
The skin to green to skin to green to skin
Green to sky
Sky to head
Head still
Green to arm 🐞 .
arm still

Child in green withdrawn
Light in green withdrawn.
To moon flickering
to lights ↑↗ to moon ˚↗
to moon with ↑↙ transverse to moon
to lights ↑↗ to moon ˚↗
to moon with ↑ transvers to bowing ←
lights scattered
to return of moon (pavilion) to scattered
lights
to transverses (leaf seg.)
to moon transversed
to moon breaking into lights colored
build to red to moon trans →
moon break to lights (artificial)
light play to moon
moon to Ala string
string to passing either, reflections,
etc.
amusement Park.

(movements of →)

Appearence of the Temple

(make mathematical — light flashes betwixt
upward and downward appearences of
temple scene)

Flare to Temple →
Bars in dark — corner flashes green →
Temple ←
Bars — (repeat) Temple → Bars ←
Temple →
Temple (distance) ←↓
Spots of children →
Temple (distance) →
Spots of children →
Temple (infantesimal) ↓↑←
Spots of children →
Light flashes + green ↑↗
Temple (infantesimal) ↑
*Light flashes + *green ↑
Light flashes + children
    (repeat)
Temple with flare to green
Green to light flashes etc. (repeat)
Temple and moon move
Temple to lines
    (Repeat Bars - Greens light flashes children)

appearence of the Temple
Proved mathematical — no light flashes

Flare to Temple →
Temple. ←
Bars to green ←→
Temple →
Bars to green →←
Lights to temple ←
Bars to green ←
Lights to ↓ Temple ←
    etc.

① white _ blue _ white _ blue
brown — blue dot — brown — moon ⊙

⌒ white noon ← noon → ↗ noon ↗ to brown
↑ moon _ →₀ _ = blue

centre ↑ moon ↑ noon ↗ noon to _ ↖ moon
_ Twice repeated sl colos stress

with → moon _ _ → ⇒ to _ ⇒→
_ Twice repeat.

with ↗ moon to _ ↖ moon ↗ ⇒ ← to _

Moon-child surred by green away down
Becoming moon
Moon emitting white lights

All white

White

White

White

White

margin alien

As early as 1956, following a Freudian trail well Frazered to Graves, I began to understand the migration of the totem thru Christ-cross to The Tree as it was to me—still very much of a mist tree as rooted in the verse previously quoted. It took a while for literary awareness to wear a way to feeling. The natural mystery of my own origins, as I was adopted, had kept both the father and mother images nebulous enough that childhood imaginings (his majesty in exile, bastard son of an international whore, found floating in a basket among the barges on the Mississippi River, creature of another planet, etc.) could project themselves into the immediate present and continue a' sending. I always tend to identify with the father of *Totem and Taboo*, especially when his stature became fully developed in *Moses and Monotheism*. The recurring dream of pursuit by the dogs intended to tear me to pieces, previously quoted, naturally brought Diana into the picture (as Rembrandt saw her, but also as Pound Cantos her), *The Golden Bough* naturally leaving me suspended with kings and virgins out on a branch very much in the dark with nothing to turn to but Graves and, as is Phoenixically natural, to the origin myth of *The White Goddess*. But setting up patriarch Freud against matriarch Graves was just foster father and mother quarreling again over golden apples.

While waiting for the grey lady to whiten in the corner, is there anything more natural than to suffer the dis-ease of Proust's protest? Asthma! Asmodeus of the Christian demonologists, known as Ashmadai to the Hebrews, back to Aeshma (as Lilith) Daeva, out of Bel (Babylonian baal) whose lady is unquestionably more Be-lit, than when Christ-crossed by almost 2000 years of virgin worship. And all those Christianly-chronic-called demons, legions and legions (did anyone ever think to ask

6 0

how many demons could sit on the head of a pin?): Asthma, Hay-Fever, Para-Hay-Fevers, Acne, Migraine, Epilepsy, etc., all scientified by Dr. Freeman (a natural pun) as Toxic Idiopathies. But the Persians knew what to say to the demon: "In truth thou art Asmodeus." And, in return, he would give a ring—teaching the sciences right down to mechanics of, etc., answering "truthfully," as well as rendering invisibility and revealing hidden treasures. Today, we can only con-verse, as Tolkien does beautifully in *The Lord of the Rings* albeit all angled out of Saxony, et cetera — "Three Rings for the Elven-kings, 7 for Dwarfs, 9 for Men, 1 for the Dark Lord."

> One Ring to rule them all, One Ring to find them,
> One Ring to bring them all and in the darkness bind them.

And "the Dark Lord?" He is (note as the lungs begin to whistle, the head to ring) the Prince of Wants. He is (mark as the familiar and recurring shape of the spot begins to spread blood color across the whole swelling area of the skin) the burn of the desire. He is (well record it in all chronicalling as you learn how the tendencies of these diseases are inherited) the god of fury, revenger-protector of "the sins of the fathers." He is (do not over-see genetic insistence as you psychologically tabulate the recurring every-day and dream-seen themes which touch off individual dis-orders) that which even assails the souls of the dead. He is that which has given the power to note, mark, record, and tabulate. He is—not...even the Indian zero becomes him. His home is (remember the visions crowding the brain as the body cripples, collapses into its foetal self) in the East— both Hesse's *Siddhartha* and Tolkien's *Journey to the East* two sides of the same coin. He is, to coin it, Revealer of—here and where-home-is his twin deceits, that an ideo-toxically-disordered individual trying to avoid the in-flict of dis-ease must, to paraphrase the prison of Dr. Freeman: avoid sun-or-other-light, seek to travel in such a manner as to inhabit only the autumnal-and-wintering seasons, shun the company of fellow human beings, sleep as little as possible, etc.—or specifically: he must cave-live, at least as one does in the concrete city, run from the hunt of the summer equinox, avoid all flowerings, sex, laughter, or other human excitements, and rest preferably in a squatting or other near wakeful position cautious to eliminate his dreams. Shall I add vice to the above? His other out is the medicinal resort: jimson weed (of the Delphic oracle) still used for colonial american asthmatics, three cigarettes (if taken in time) providing adequate vascular constriction to stop my spring-summery-morning attacks while weakening the lungs for the following morning. Westward Ho, technological man! The world is a ring that brings you round. But spite of all this, I direct the mind eastward, blind mine eyes, and so know and use "the Dark Lord" as Blake knew and used him...as even Solomon used him to build the Temple.

An actor of some of my earlier films, Newcomb by name, visited my wife and me at Ides of March, 1960, we very much inhabiting that time-place then. He, having once portrayed my false mask: curiosity (out of Yeats' *A Vision*): was now slowly working his own way thru *Shadow Garden* and listening for cues. Mid night he was awakened by the howling of cats. There grew in the corner of the room of his mind a large white tree triple branched to the ceiling whose roots, naturally, never touched the floor. The tree, all of the garden, aglow, phosphorescent in the night as naturally as veins standing blue on the white wrist, was a moving image...that is, of and in an approach to the new. As he moved to ward it, i.e., to prove it a painted image of some filmic contrivance, ieeeeee, it danced in interrelationship with all his motion, was distinct from the wall (the viewer fixing stance in relation to the wall, the distinction being twixt The Tree and The Wall) yet could be seen thru to the wallflowers in and of that dance (the mind's eye given thus its glass, the choice between image-zen-ations monocle and/or some more westerly wonder-ring.) Newcomb turned to the windows, searched their panes for explanatory cracks, perhaps reflecting moonlight, found himself on the dark side of the house and, in dark of moon, returned to bed...to blanket himself under cover. The next morning at breakfast all his vision became incident which excited both my wife and myself at the time but we promptly, obeying our own cues, forgot. Proceeding truly with our life all before us, I dragged a dead white tree up two-thirds of a mountain, re-planted it so that my wife could photograph my actor-self pushing it down and chopping it into the fragments of material for my epic film *Dog Star Man*. That took us to the almost, uninhabitable time-space of mid-summer, where-when curiosity became my motivating force, and I sought out my actor of the vision. I proceeded to remember and fix with referential hypo our physical-space habitation of that time: that we had then been living in a community called Silver Spruce, Star Route, Boulder Canyon, accessible only by crossing a bridge clearly marked by the Colo. Dept. of Highways "DI5AN," all water passing east down the canyon from Nederland Dam. My cat self out of the bag proceeded to spend its nine moon-given lives at an astonishing rate, one asthma attack after another sending me to the hospital. We found ourselves living in a city of the plains where we had moved at the begin of summering, the circle of equals. We found our love dying by inches, all measurement reduced to interstices, all attraction of opposites pulled to taught with study, all past tense to trap—or, in other words: all of net. And as in prophet, the brood of thoughts shaped a vast dream body (Jonathan Williams once asking: "What is the plural of cosmos ?") turning in its sleep as I turned in mine (as Otto Rank and Artaud can both dream oppositely of the same "double") its movements corresponding exactly to mine but mimed as an unact of alphabetical action (as naturally as Wittgenstein destroyed the picture-theory of language to create the riddle in which "the riddle does not exist") therefore moving as if with centuries of imperceptible s-pace (thought of as Michael McClure thought of his child's first sounds: "Art is Zen") and perceived to be moving from in to im balance in my awakening. In the daytime I lifted the tons of stone of the Graveyard of Père Lachaise, now transparent two-dimensional image-film-stripped, and ordered this lyre of the originals. In the evening a man named Sigismund visited preparing the sacrificial rite: "...to be opened...the hands up-turned on the knees ...the legs apart...the breathing deep and steady...the eyes attuned to the inward sound...the eyes fixed to the single object of concentration...turned in ward...turned in...side...out...;" and the approach to the altar: "to receiving...fingers entwined ...hands clasped behind the back...to prevent one from touching the spirit vision...to be prepared to be touched by the spirit force without reciprocation...to speak when spoken to and never to interrupt the voice of the vision...to stand aside and never block or cast human shadow on the view...to approach from the out...side...in..." And in a darkened room lit only by red-light, havoc on the optic nerves, the spiritually lazy gathered demanding their rite, evoking only the spirits of the plains, caterwauling unrehearsed hymns and pop tunes to fabricate ectoplasm, boxing vox to the noises of the medium, behind his curtain, and indians, "ugh," and Ethyl Barrymore, "my dears," appeared as the medium-curtailed night-curtain came down, sinking all into the Styx. A siamese cat led me out of the ceremoaning, till only its distant ecto ringed my ears, led me out of Knighthood into the night, its dark form a black to match Yeats' sky so white "a child might think" "a spot of ink" could destroy it; and I saw, by its undreamed stars, the turn of all my mind. Later that night, camera once again in hand I photographed an eclipse of the moon. In this fall, we moved away from astral and geographical plains back to Star Route mountains in ghost town Crisman, to finish with *The Dead* and to continue in pursuit of the Dog Star Man.

I evolved in some nonsuch as the belief that visualization had limited itself to illustration until this century (for whatever) reason had been the binding (forever) the poetic word the texture (ever) and the picture the graphic of the book of the world; and I proceeded to search for The Tree among the card catalogues (other elements of all creation myth: dragon-serpent-dog, star-man-and-twin-self-Hercules-Dionysus, and woman-triplicate-or-nine-fold, readily libraried) and I found it missing. And then, coming again to Pound in the earliest of *Personae*, "...stood still and was a tree amid the wood." Touching on Villier of the isle of Adam, I found key to the missing linked age binding tree to the background of all sets, at least since "The Dream of The Rood" of the Savior's Tree over-shadowed Kynon's tale in The Romances from the Cycle of King Arthur, i.e., since the tree stripped of leaves learned to sing of itself, "adorned with silver and gold," to boast, "I could have crushed them all. And yet I kept myself erect," and with self-piy, "I bear the scars of malicious gashes," in identification with Christ, "we were both reviled, we two together," since its earlier upbringing out of Jewish parentage, "reared as a cross" obscures The Tree of Owain's quest which, when stripped of leaves, is clothed in vision of new spring: "Great flocks of multicolored birds lighted upon the tree and sang, covering its bare branches, a melodious foliage." And with Kai, I could agree, "I never heard any melody equal to that, either before or since," until I imagined the singing of the woodman in the distance as Axel destroyed the twin luring illusions of sexual love and hidden treasure. Then Santa Claus became real again as L. Frank Baum found him "Child of the Forest" becoming "Woodsman," or as Tolkien's Strider becoming Aragorn, Beorn becoming Bombadill, *The Hobbit* becoming part of *The Fellowship of The Ring*. And by way of "Distances" I came to sighting "Variations" with Charles Olson while "In Cold Hell, In Thicket," or at times to handspring "thru a barrier of 'em" with Michael McClure singing "Hymns to St. Geryon" and finally to attending Robert Duncan's "Opening of the Field." And so to The Woman, Jane going on to become Virgin Mary Crazy Jane Mad-onna Jenny, even memorizing Broughtonian drama, played it out as I sought, by way of Shelley to come "To Jane With A Guitar," fashioned of the wood of the tree. In loss of this, in less of Jane with all miss-myth, I often thought to go with Stevenson's axeman, "to die with Odin," and began a lec-tourmg round the country, even became entrepreneur for bringing poets to the sad state of Colorado, soon becoming public imaged Dog-Star-Ad-Man-Oroborus, reducible to even TV's eyes, chewing tales and otherwise making the scene, interfering with seeing—as I'm here-doing …to be un-doing. To begin then in fall, where all name dropping accompanies, with Broughton's "A Prelude for Brakhage:"

> I saw in the frame
> the cosmic game
> of all that begins and ends,
> I saw the whole screen
> of turbulent dream
> from which the world descends.
>
> I saw on the sky
> a human eye
> in search of angelic friends.
> I saw in the frame
> a man's heart aflame
> with all that begins and ends.

and then, from Chamælirium luteum, yet true friend restored, six months later in answer to further quest shunning:

> "Let it be"*

After which the rest was wind-wise taken out of hand, in moment of recognition, and sailed into a nearby stream heading seaward. And then from Michael McClure an angry action re: previous chapters of *Metaphors on Vision*:

(Grumble...snarl...) I believe that one of the social functions of the artist is to destroy constantly such ideas as myth and ritual—or any other habitual and accustomed 'vision.' Clyfford Still said it perfectly long ago—look at the quote of his I use in the first Hymn to St. Geryon—right after THE GESTURE, THE GESTURE...**

reminding me immediately, I only looking-up Still later, of:

ONE PERCEPTION MUST IMMEDIATELY AND DIRECTLY LEAD TO A FURTHER PERCEPTION.

and of that entire section of Charles Olson's *Statements on Poetics* which most perfectly describes for me the working processes which have come increasingly into their own thru each attempt on my part while filming and editing to avoid John's Cage, per chance, these last several years. Per Se:

Olson's (the passage referred to above.)

"...the process of the thing, how the principle can be made so to shape the energies that the form is accomplished. And I think it can be boiled down to one statement (first pounded into my head by Edward Dahlberg): ONE PERCEPTION MUST IMMEDIATELY AND DIRECTLY LEAD TO A FURTHER PERCEPTION. It means exactly what it says, is a matter of, at all points (even, I should say, of our management of daily reality as of the daily work) get on with it, keep moving, keep in speed, the nerves, their speed, the perceptions, theirs, the acts, the split second acts, the whole business, keep it moving as fast as you can, citizen."***

Cage's (selected from *Silence* by chance operations)

"The highest purpose is to have no purpose at all. This puts one in accord with nature in her manner of operation. If someone comes along and asks why?, there are answers. However there is a story I have found very helpful. What's so interesting about technique anyway? *What if there are twelve tones in a row?* What row? This seeing of cause and effect is not emphasized but instead one makes an identification with what is here and now. He then spoke of two qualities. Unimpededness and Interpenetration.

The relationship of things happening at the same time is spontaneous and irrepressible.
It is you yourself
in the form you have
that instant taken.
To stop and figure it out
takes time."

and then, of principal, from *Figure of Outward*, Robert Creeley:

FORM IS NEVER MORE THAN
AN EXTENSION OF CONTENT.

or, as in detail, in a letter:

> Ah well! But really your films, you see, showed me how
> detail can be invested with a rhythmic insistence apart
> from an overt 'meaning' for 'purpose' etc. That is, see-
> ing your films I do see, first of all, and 'think' later—
> and that's what I'm now intent to accomplish as a
> ground sense in the narrative. So that I write what
> 'comes to mind,' rather than what I might propose
> should 'come to mind' etc. So that the control comes in
> finding just that sense of the thing provoked by its 'ap-
> pearance' in the narrative, be it a sudden anecdote, or
> simply the insistent feeling that a sense of relation is at
> the given moment best said as 'an empty ice box' etc. I
> want in short to give over the process of 'explanation'
> and/or 'understanding' of a specious kind—

And finally then, from Robert Duncan, on "depth" and
"complexity":

> Given the immediate frame of the film, or 'word' of
> the poem—the perspective or history arises to express
> the felt-known content of the frame. For painter and
> poet (and then won't it be true for film maker?) this is
> his imagination of what a man, a tree, a river, God,
> past, or form is, and depends upon, springs from his
> area of intent in living. If he have taken deep thought
> —what we call study (as Charles Olson studies the na-
> ture and. origins of language and action)—then he will
> need depth: his imperatives will come from those
> depths. If he have complex recognitions (as Proust or
> Shakespeare) then the art finds the medium complex.

and in an earlier letter:

> If I've tried to get one idea across in the art it is that the
> poet must have no deep and complex feelings, no 'I' at

all that does not belong to, arise in the orders of, the poem itself.****

And of the film itself, as I then wrote:

(I mean the strips of film and what moves me of what's been to begin to splice what is to be, or ((if I hesitate)) thru its insistence upon what has to be)

and its relationship to all this period of (sigh)-arc-(eeoh)-phi-(fie-fiddle-eoh)-(so)-seesaw-med-Id-(EEEEEEE)-The-awl-(lowww)-pose-poe-rhet-(eeeeee)-call-spir-(i.e.)(tummmmm), refer to the title of this chapter, and sentence. The self again to the para-noidal-graph of round's-stance, for it is a game played here too Siriusly for comfort, myself having here the last word in this beginning, all played out in tent of living, "an empty ice box," per-chance-perception gestating all this tour which when working howsomever being then whom?-soever with whatever lets it be. Most often then, when taking a break and margined to most living room, Gertrude Stein comes to me, "In the great kitchen of my fanciful world," as Sherwood Anderson saw her, sits down at the table, throws back her head, "As if staring straight into the face of the sun," as Donald Sutherland saw her, and sings. And all questions of relay-(myth-rit-or-other-wise) are lost in choiring, all religious becoming:

Mountains and mountains of saints singing and singing

and I am delighted, of light air breathing; and all dark lording it over is over, leaving only super-stich for a thread of Proustian "dress-making," and that too passing into remembrance and out of immediacy of experienced singing:

I am not I when I see

or laughing down all criti-cat-calling and The-arising:

Oh, praise, praise, praise!

making margin without alien:

And now I am truly false if with this ending, back to all beginnings. Is this then but another ring with which to bind 'em?; all these pages so much mumblety for such unchivalric pegging?; am I still in-flu with now Steinian spiritus anti-bodying?; will I will out with mu-sick, testamentioning the Ruggled-Ivesy-covered-Weberning-Cage-of-a-Stockhausen, making a paraphrase of Varèse because his name, like all else of him, won't fit a metaphorical line-up, drowning St. Subotnick 'clause to all the new sound word ear rationals such as Tenney-Sender-Mumma-Young-and-Ashley-Krumm, (and where-e-ohwhere'll Berio go), and what has it all to do with Ann Arbor, St. Francis, and enfantterrible York?; and would I do better to say "Zen," moan "A," pursue the water-lillies spreading Pollock in the air and follow thru the process to "deK"?; or would a soundring influenzing describe a film more filmically than script, than art, than arc-key, than spin-spherically?; and is a film, a fil, a fi-fie-foe-fiddle-di-dum?

A Post Script

Three nights ago I decided to stop righting. Later, when I turned in somnia, the darkened room full filled itself with growing branches glowing white which, when thought of as related to Michael McClure's "cracks of brightness," Laman-tia's "Weir," Anglo-Saxon "Aelf-Scin," all faded, died to the eyes, leaving me once again in the dark. Thus, the last several hundred words since the last word of ended ritual, a "Beware the Dog" who might go as I have here into the House of the Poet, the Seance, Sancti-or-scientified, knik-knacking and knocking about, looking for keys and key-rings, symbols, sturms and drangsss, et sets. I am thru writing, thru writing. It is only as of use as useless.

NOTES

*(The whole Broughton poem had to be fished for downstream among the rocks and rapids:

> Let it be.
> Let me be
> here by the sea
> like the boatman I saw in Bangkok
> smiling by the sunrise river
> as he washes,
> as he pours over himself
> a bucket of the river,
> pours over and over himself
> the river to which he has offered
> his spit, his urine, his shit,
> the river which he drinks and launders in —
> pours it over himself
> with a smile
> as he washes —
> and then sits down refreshed
> and starts fishing.

**(The statement by Clyfford Still as quoted by Michael McClure in his first Hymn to St. Geryon): *Clyfford Still:* "We are committed to an unqualified act, not illustrating outworn myths or contemporary alibis. One must accept total responsibility for what he executes. And the measure of his greatness will be the depth of his insight and courage in realizing his own vision. Demands for communication are presumptuous and irrelevant."

***Continuation of the paragraph from Charles Olson's "Statements on Poetics" quoted previously: "And if you also set up as a poet, USE USE USE the process at all points, in any given poem always, always one perception must must **MOVE, INSTANTER, ON ANOTHER!**"

****(Or to be extremely specific, reguarding against ((as Robert Creeley would call it)) "specious" usage of language by filmmakers or other—from a yet earlier letter from Robert Duncan): "Feelings take on depth and complexity *only* in language—these are terms of the articulation itself."

SELECTIONS FROM
brakhage
scrapbook

make place for the artist

This is to introduce myself. I am young and I believe in magic. I am learning how to cast spells. My profession is transforming. I am what is known as an "artist." Three years ago I made a discovery which caused me dis-ease at the time: neither the society in which I had grown up nor my society at that moment, my college, knew what to do with me. They were wary of me.

I, suddenly without inheritance, began a three year adventure to seek the fortune of myself. This information is for professors wondering over an age of introspective art. Some say that no one has ever known what to do with the artist until after he is dead. Then his body is disposed of and his life works are buried in museums and libraries and, sometimes, in men's minds

As over half of the culture professors of this and every other college campus earn their living from picking the bones of the dead, it is hoped they will be interested in the flesh of their future. This is a living artist speaking. It is a re-quest which brings me back to Dartmouth at this time. This is a state meant.

I am presenting it in writing for someone else's future. Someone may someday realize that the living artist has the eyes of the age he lives in. They may understand that he makes his magic for the moment. Who knows? Here's what to do:

Make place for the artist. Do it now. For you, as well as him, tomorrow is too late. First must come understanding, not of the work but of the worker. Give him the right conditions. Here are the conditions. This breed requires freedom. Cages kill him. Restrictions constrict. This animal is forever at war with his own limitations by nature. The rules others try to impose usually only baffle and, finally, either destroy or else disinherit him.

The artist must be given more than enough rope. He often hangs himself for the experience, however this creature has a tough neck, give him time! He is perhaps more aware of time than any other type of individual. He is an explorer of his own dualities. He embarks on as many adventures as there are in a day. These are the components of his witch brew.

It takes time, also, to stir up a magic potion. Information for opportunists—the best way to get something from an artist is to leave him alone. Contradiction is part of the honesty he exercises. It is impossible for any man to express without contradicting himself every other statement and be anything but a liar, unless he is playing a part. The artist plays his part best apart.

It is because this college has a tradition of individuality that I speak so frankly. I have, during the last three years, uncovered many radical art schools with much display of individuality but no foundation for keeping it alive. Their fires are explosive but they frizzle quickly. I believe that Dartmouth has coals unturned.

Perhaps I'm no match for it. I am a match that would like to ignite without being consumed. My words have turned up a circle, and I'm back to ideas I had when I first arrived in Hanover three and a half years ago.

It was a liberal education I wanted. I was, and am, alive with more curiosity than it would be possible for any man to satisfy in a lifetime. A college was expected to save me time in my investigations, but it was not dreamed of that time would be saved by pre-digesting those investigations.

I was barraged with a tangle of facts and given no time to unite them. The explorer will never be satisfied by the motion pictures of the expedition. I had assumed that a liberal education would be taught liberally to everyone according to his individual inclination.

I had expected there would be time for keeping the fires burning under the magic potion. Instead there was only an endless series of pot-boilers to be warmed over. The smoke dreams of the artist are as necessary to his well being as the air he breathes.

Make place for the artist, Dartmouth, for he is the most demanding but at the same time the most generous of all the individuals your tradition might speak for. He is the fire for a living theater under the hands of your great drama professors. He is the dream of your inspiring professors of literature.

He can make use of their inspiration. He can give you a literary quarterly worth keeping. He is the unheard sound of your musical department. He can give your instruments new notes to play. He is what your artists in residence are residing for. He can make your screens alive with your own cinema images. He must never be used as material. Those who try to hold fire either burn their hands or put the fire out.

This is a hair of the dog, given with love and expectation.

[1955]

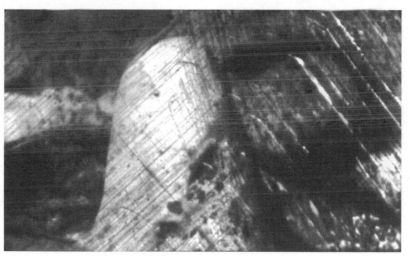

Thigh Line Lyre Triangular

film and music

Dear Ronna Page,

Jonas Mekas will have whatever material has been salvaged on and/or by me—old clips, "stills," etcetera—as I make a practice of sending them all to him for Film-Makers' Cooperative files.

As to quotes out of my past, I imagine you have ample material in *Film Culture* issues and my book *Metaphors on Vision*. I am presently working on a long film (16mm) to be called: *Scenes from Under Childhood*. It would probably be of particular interest to your Parisian readers to know that this work-in-progress is to some extent inspired by the music of Olivier Messiaen and, to some lesser extent, Jean Barraque, Pierre Boulez, Henri Pousseur, and Karlheinz Stockhausen (all, I believe, former pupils of Messiaen).

Fifteen years ago I began working with the film medium as primarily shaped by the influence of stage drama. Since that time, both poetry and painting have alternately proved more growth-engendering sources of inspiration than either the trappings of the stage or the specific continuity limitation of any "making up a story," novelistic tendencies, etcetera: and the first departures in my working-orders from "fiction" sources gave rise to an integral involvement with musical notation as a key to film editing aesthetics. Some ten years ago I studied informally with both John Cage and Edgard Varèse, at first with the idea of searching out a new relationship between image and sound and, thus, creating a new dimension for the sound track, as Jean Isidore Isou's *Venom and Eternity* had created in me a complete dissatisfaction with the conventional usages of music for "mood" and so-called "realistic sounds" as mere referendum to image in movies, and Jean Cocteau's poetic film plays, for all their dramatic limitations, had demonstrated beautifully to me that only non-descriptive language could co-exist with moving image (in any but a poor operatic sense), that words, whether spoken or printed could only finally relate to visuals in motion thru a necessity of means and/or an integrity as severely visual as that demonstrated by the masterpieces of collage.

The more informed I became with aesthetics of sound, the less I began to feel any need for an audio accompaniment of the visuals I was making. I think it was seven/eight years ago I began making *intentionally* silent films. Although I have always kept myself open to the possibilities of sound while creating any film, and in fact made a number of sound films these last several years, I now see/feel no more absolute necessity for a sound track than a painter feels the need to exhibit a painting with a recorded musical background. Ironically, the more silently-oriented my creative philosophies have become, the more inspired-by-music have my photographic aesthetics and my actual editing orders become, both engendering a coming into being of the physiological relationship between seeing and hearing in the making of a work of art in film.

I find, with Cassius Keyser, that "the structure of mathematics is similar to that of the human nervous system" and have for years been studying the relationship between physiology and mathematics via such books as Sir D'Arcy Thompson's *On Growth and Form*: and following those "leads" along a line of music, I've come to the following thoughts (which I'll quote from an article of mine which appeared in the magazine *Wild Dog*): "I'm somehow now wanting to get deeper into my concept of music as sound equivalent of the mind's moving, which is becoming so real to me that I'm coming to believe the study of the history of music would reveal more of the changing thought processes of a given culture than perhaps any other means—not of thought shaped and/or Thoughts but of the *Taking shape,* physiology of thought or some such... I mean, is there anything that will illustrate the feel of chains of thought gripping and ungripping, rattling slowly around, a block-con-

cept, an Ideal, as Gregorian chant, for instance?...and doesn't
The Break occur in Western musical thought in terms of melody,
story, carrying blocks, making them events, along a line? (Or, as
poet Robert Kelly put it to me recently: "& event is the greatness
of story, i.e., where story & history & myth & mind & physiology *all* at once interact"—and events as they enter each other in
the act, in the course, of the line of melody? (I'm reminded here
that Gregorian notes WERE blocks in manuscript, stems attached
later to make flowers of 'em, and then, still later, strung along
lined paper, etcetera. And sometime later, when the notes were
well rounded, flowering right-and-upside-down, sporting flags,
holes, etc., and all planted in the neat gardens of the page, all in
rows, it was possible for Mozart to play Supreme Gardener; but
there lurked Wagner who would, did, make of each line of
melody a block, specifically referential, so that the French could
image melody as a landscape, all thought referential to picture,
i.e. to something OUTside the musical frame of reference. But
then Webern made of it a cube, all lines of melody converging
on some center to form a cluster or what composer James Tenney,
writing about Varese, does call "a Klang." And it does seem to
me that with John Cage we are, thru chance operations, to some
approximation of Gregorian Chant again—not held to links, as
of a chain-of-thought, but rather to the even more rigid mathematical bell-shaped curve."

J. S. Bach has been called "the greatest composer of the 20th
century": his current popularity is probably due to the facts that
(1) he was the greatest composer of his own time and (2) most
of the western world has, in the meantime, come to think *easily*
in a baroque fashion—come to think *naturally* baroquely, one
might say were it not that this process of thought is the result of
these several centuries of cultural training. The most modern
baroqueists in music were, of course, the twelve-tonists: and my
Anticipation of the Night was specifically inspired by the relationships I heard between the music of J. S. Bach and Anton

Webern. The crisis of Western Man's historical thought processes struggling with the needs of contemporary living (technological as against mechanistic) has never been more clearly expressed than in Webern's adaptation of Bach's *Musical Offering* (which piece has inspired several films of mine, most dramatically the sound film *Blue Moses*): but the most essentially optimistic (if I may use so psychological a word) force of musical thought has come from Debussy, Faure, Ravel, Roussel, Satie, and even Lili Boulanger, etcetera—all moving along a line of hearing into the inner ear (the sphere of "music of the spheres" being now *consciously* the human head)...just as all visual masters of this century who've promised more than a past-tension of The Illustrative have centered the occasions of their inspiration in the mind's eye (so-called "Abstract Painting" having a very *concrete* physiological basis in "closed eye vision").

I seek to hear color just as Messiaen seeks to see sounds. As he writes (in notes for the record of *Chronochromie*).

Colour: the sounds *colour* the durations because they are, for me, bound to colour by unseen ties.

I find these "ties" to be sense impulses of the nervous system and find them to have exact physiological limitations but unlimited psychological growth potential thru the act of seeing and hearing, and/or otherwise sensing, them. Messiaen goes on:

When I listen to music, and even when I read it, I have an inward vision of marvellous colours — colours which blend like combinations of notes, and which shift and revolve with the sounds.

I recall first hearing shifting chords of sound that corresponded in meaningful interplay with what I was seeing when I was a child in a Kansas cornfield at mid-night. That was the first time I was in an environment *silent* enough to permit me to hear "the music of the spheres," as it's called, and visually specific enough for me to be aware of the eye's pulse of receiving image.

John Cage once, in a soundproof chamber, picked out a dominant fifth and was told later that he was hearing his nervous system and blood circulation: but the matter is a great deal more complicated than that—at least as much more complicated as the whole range of musical chord possibilities is to the, any, dominant fifth...for instance, any tone of the inner-ear seems to be hearable as a pulse, or wave of that tone, or *irregular* rhythm and tempo, "waveringness" one might say: and yet these hearable pulse-patterns *repeat,* at intervals, and reverse, and et cetera, in a way analogous to the "themes and variation" patterns of some western musical forms. External sounds heard seem to affect these inner-ear pulses *more* by way of the emotions engendered than by specific tonal and/or rhythmic correspondences: whereas the external pulse perceived by the eye does seem to more directly affect the ear's in-pulse. But then that's a much more complicated matter, too, because the eye has its own in-pulse—the color red, for instance, will be held, with the eye closed, as a retention-color with a much different vibrancy, or pulse, than red seems with eyes open, and so on—and the rhythm-pattern-flashes of the eye's nerve-ends, making up the grainy shapes of closed-eye vision, are quite distinct from inner-ear's "theme and variations"...so much so that no familiar counterpoint is recognizable. Well, just so—for these fields of the mind feeling out its own physiology via eyes and ears turned inward, so to speak, are prime centers of inspiration for both musical and visual composers of this century who take Sense as Muse (as do all who recognize the move from Technological to Electrical Era of 20th century living)...and there is very little historical precedence in the working orders, or the achievements, of these artists.

Well, all of the above essaying (which grew way beyond any intended length) should at least serve to distinguish my intentions and processes, and whatever films of mine arise therethru, from most of the rest of the so-called Underground Film

Movement: and (as you asked specifically about this in your letter) I'll take the opportunity to emphasize that I feel at polar odds and ends therefrom whatever usually arises from that "movement" into public print, especially when journalists and critics are presuming to write about myself and my work. I'm certainly nothing BUT uneasy about the any/everybody's too facile sense of mixed-media, which seems by report to be dominating the New York Scene, at the present. Whether the "mix" is per chance (operations) or per romance (opera) or per some scientific stance (Op) or just plain folksy, Grand Ol' Opry, dance (Pop), I've very little actual interest in it, nor in The Old Doc-(umentary) school, with its "spoon full of sugar help the medicine go down" either—all these socio-oriented effect-films being related to "The Cause" rather than Aesthetics...and some of them, naturally, working beautifully in that context; but most of them, these days causing sensibility-crippling confusions in the long run, because all are sailing into import under the flag of "Art," leaving that term bereft of meaning and those films which are simply "beautiful works" (which will "do no work" but will "live forever," as Ezra Pound says of his songs) lacking the distinction that there IS that possibility for cinema, as established in all other arts, or works that *can* and *must* be seen many times, *will* last, *have* qualities of integrality to be shored against the dis-continuities of fashionable time. I do not ever like to see a "Cause" *made* of, or around, a work of art; and I strive to make films integrally cohesive enough to be impregnable to the rape of facile usage (shudder at the thought of Hitler shoveling eight million Jews into the furnace off the pages of *Thus Spake Zarathustra*, et cetera, for instance).

To be clear about it (and to answer another of your questions about my attitude toward increasing censorship): I've many times risked jail sentences for showing films of mine which were, at the time, subject to sexual censorship laws, and will do so again if the occasion arises: but I *have never,* and *will*

never, force said works upon an unprepared or antagonistic audience, have never made them party-to/subject-of
(and/or) /illustration-for "The Cause of Sexual Freedom" or
some-such. I made those films, as all my films, out of *personal*
necessity taking shape thru means available to me of historical
aesthetics. I risked imprisonment showing them in order to meet
the, as requested, needs of others. To have *forced* these works
upon others, because of my presumption of the good-for-them
in such occasion, would have been to blaspheme against the process out of which the works arise and to have eventually destroyed myself as instrument of that process...freedom, of
expression-or-other, can only exist meaningfully out of full respect to the means of its becoming: and a work of art does
never impress, in the usual sense of the word, but rather is free-
express always—and it does, therefore, require some free space,
some fragile atmosphere of attenuated sensibility, in which to
be received...the social strength of the arts is rooted in human
need to freely attend, which demonstrates itself over and over
again in that people finally DO create such an UNlikely (free of
all likenesses) space wherein aesthetic (shaped with respect to
his/somebody else's and history's means) can be received. Let
society's sex-pendulum swing "anti" again, if it will (tho' I hope
it won't), the works of art of sex impulse will continue to be
made as surely as babies and to have an eventual public life as
surely as babies grow up.

[1966]

a moving picture giving
and taking book

This is a moving picture giving and taking book. It will begin with those areas of moving pictures where the gift of the maker is most easily accomplished, and move toward those areas where taking is predominant—but always with the view in my mind of encouraging giving...my sense of accomplishment being determined by the extent to which the moving picture maker can continue to *give* when increased technical knowledge permits him to *take* more and more from and of moving pictures, bless him.

I begin with very few assumptions about you, reader, but I must presume some interest on your part in becoming a moving picture maker; and I'll refer to you as maker, for short, and for the long view of your historical origin (as instrument of giving of yourself) in *the poet*. I'll thank you not to presume on this title — I invoke it to help inspire the writing of this book...I leave it to the powers of your being to determine whether or not you have and/or will have earned it. Thank you.

I assume that you have no tools for moving picture making, and I must begin, now, to ask of you. Provide yourself with a strip of moving picture film. It may be called 8 *millimeter (mm,* for short), 16mm, 35mm, or any other mm#, so long as it has the kind of holes in it which make it possible to move it and thus make moving pictures of it. The film may be:

This book is dedicated to Michael McClure, who spoke to me of the need for a short book on film technique which could be read by poets; and Bobbie Creeley, who gave me a beautiful sense of Home in her home-movie making; and Joan Kelly, who made me aware of the word-root of *amateur,* and so, *with love,* SB

(I) *Black Leader* (Unexposed and developed film——opacity: the result of retained emulsion.)

Note whatever other color the black is tinged with: brown, usually, or if color-film-black-leader: blue, green, etc. (Sometimes referred to as Opaque Leader) note it is not opaque, how much light passes thru it, how it can be seen thru.

(2) *Clear Leader* (Exposed and developed film—clarity: the result of the removal of emulsion.)

Note whatever color its clarity is tinged with: blue, purple, yellow, etc. (Sometimes referred to as Blank Leader) note it is not blank, how many dust motes, scratches, imperfections dot its surface and interfere with the transmission of light.

(3) *White Leader* (Unexposed and undeveloped film—it has been fixed: hypoed.)

Note whatever other color the white is tinged with: yellow, usually, etc. (Sometimes referred to simply as Leader) this is the material most often used at the beginning of a film to be pro-jected.

(4) *Gray Leader* (Unexposed and undeveloped *and* unhypoed film.)

Note whatever other color its grayness is tinged with: usually deep purple, etc. Note also its possible color changes as it sits exposed to the light day after day.

(5) *Moving pics*

Which, I assume, you didn't take but an interest in, perhaps only to the extent that they were given you free of even the small cost of the above-mentioned leaders.

Your strip of film will, in all cases, have a dull side and a shiny side (tho' you will find it difficult to tell the difference if using clear leader). The shiny side will be referred to as *the base side,* and the dull side will be referred to as *the emulsion side* (which accounts for your difficulty with clear leader from which almost all emulsion has been removed—tho' the emulsion side still remains stickier when moistened than the base side). I will now ask you to make some marks upon the emulsion side of the strip: (if you have either black leader or gray leader, I suggest you scratch the emulsion side of the film with some sharp instrument of your own choice)—(if you have clear leader I suggest you use india ink applied with some point suitable for making both small dots and fairly even lines)—(if you have any of the other types of strips of film listed above, I encourage either scratching or inking and/or both if you choose)…please do not be inhibited by my suggestions as they are only offered with specific reference to forthcoming text—that is, if you are excited enough, at this time, lay aside this book and go to work. And good luck to you if this is our parting point.

Your strip of film will have a series of evenly spaced rectangular holes punched along either one or both sides of it: these will be referred to as *sprocket holes.* Film with sprocket holes on both sides will be referred to as *double-sprocketed*—film sprocketed on only one side: *single-sprocketed.* Hold the strip so that it dangles, vertically, down. With double-sprocketed film, the space between each set of double sprockets (or, in single-sprocketed film, that space you can define if you imagine an identical set of sprocket holes on the side opposite of those you have) is the *picture area*—that is, each set of sprocket holes defines the area of an individual, unmoving, transparent picture…and when you hold the strip vertically, with its emulsion side facing you, it is in position for the correct projection of a series of individual, unmoving, images of exactly what you see on the film when looking thru each window defined by sprocket holes (except that, in order to project the image you see, to enlarge it brightly and sharply on some distant plane, you would have to concentrate bright light thru it and focus it sharply thru some lens which would, given an average lens, reverse left to right and vice versa, but *not*, ordinarily, top to bottom). If you focus your own eyes sharply upon it, you will notice irregularities in whatever kind of film strip you hold, in even the most so-called opaque or blank; and these nicks or scratches in black, dust motes and hairs in clear, etc., are, given controlled light and a lens, eminently projectionable (tho' usually considered objectionable) pictures. Similarly, any mark you make, whether scratched, inked, or both, can be projected *(and objective—dependent on your thoughtfulness, the precision of your mark, and your precise knowledge of the picture area which will be projected—so to be both more precise and, of necessity, general about it: the top and bottom lines of your frame,* as picture area is also called, can be imagined as equally dividing the sprocket holes on either side, the right and left framing as continuing the inside vertical line established by the sprocket holes...tho' generally, this picture area is dependent upon the projector, etc., so that all edges of your frame are somewhat indeterminate). Now you, the maker, are qualified to make still images for projection; and all those interested in making black and white, hand-drawn, slide films can discontinue reading this book.

And now it is time for a story. I do not know whether it is a true story, in the sense of fact; but it is certainly true in a mythic sense...and it is wonderful that so young a medium as motion picture making already has its myths. It is said that Pathé, great 19th century inventor and photographer, invited his friend Méliès, a famous stage magician, over to his house to show him a new gadget he'd created. He projected onto the wall a picture of a beach scene with incoming waves. Méliès must have fidgeted, as image-projection, or transparencies, were nothing new to him (did, in fact, date back centuries to the undetermined origin of shadow-plays); but suddenly the waves in that image began to move, were actually seen coming in to splash dramatically on the beach (and these moving projections were not mere shadow silhouettes in movement but composed of photographic detail). Méliès must immediately have taken the phenomenon as Magic, and then as "magic" in his business sense of the word; for, so the story goes, he at once tried to buy whatever gadget produced this effect, and then he asked how it worked, etc. But Pathé would neither sell his marvelous gadget nor would he reveal the secret of its workings; for he said that, to his way of thinking, moving pictures were not for entertainment but for serious scientific purposes and to be used only as a recording device, etc. So, Méliès went home and, simply out of his knowledge of transparencies, and his realization that they were capable of moving picture transformations, created a motion picture projector of his own. As I find the origin, or at least the mythological origin, of all moving picture making, other than as defined by Pathé's way of thinking, in this stage magician Méliès, I will refer to him often—of which this is an introduction...to be engendering a: how did he do?

As I am assuming that you have no moving picture camera, I suggest you draw, by ink or by scratch, some representation of Pathé's beach scene as you imagine it; and as you are probably finding the fingernail size picture area somewhat restrictive, I further suggest that you draw, however sketchily, a single incoming wave. Move down the strip of film one frame and redraw your wave as exactly like the one in the frame above as you are able, only make it a little, very little, more incoming—very slightly closer to whichever edge of the frame its crest is pointing. Move down to the third frame and repeat this process, drawing-in your wave a little further. Et cetera. If you choose to become elaborate, you might attempt to draw, in each succeeding frame, some simulation of the increasing collapse of your wave upon some beach or other of your imagination; but this would probably require a more careful study of ocean waves, if you have an ocean available, than you have ever before imagined. In any case, you have now begun the creation of a potentially movable picture universe of your giving. It is a simpler matter for you to set your universe in motion than it was for either God or Méliès, for there are a number of machines ready-made to engage with your basic material, the strip of film, and to automatically project the gift of your incoming wave to a distant enlargement, *and* to project the whole series of waves in such a way as to give them the appearance of being a single wave in movement. These machines can be divided into two types: *moving picture projectors* and *moving picture viewers*. But before I introduce you to these two types, and the various kinds of machine within each category, I would like to make you familiar with the essential process which is common to all so that no matter which kind or type of machine you encounter you will always be able to engage it with whatever film strip you have for the most successful marriage of the two in operation and the simplest possible birth of moving pictures.

If you were drawing on paper, as indeed Méliès must first have done, rather than a strip of moving picture film, as instructed, I would have asked you to make each drawing of your wave on a different sheet of paper and then to have flipped rapidly through the whole sequence to produce a moving picture. This is indeed, an adequate method with which to practice sequential drawing and serves to illustrate three aspects of the moving picture process:

(1) What you can most readily notice from thumbing thru flippics is that the success of the illusion of movement depends most critically upon the flips: those split-second interruptions between pictures, when one picture has vanished in the blur of the page turning and

the next picture has not yet become fully visible—were it not for those interruptions between pictures the pics themselves would blur into an unintelligible mass of lines.

(2) You can also note that the timing of the flipping, or flip-rhythm, is crucial—when flipped too slowly, the series reveals itself to be exactly what it is: a series of still pictures…when flipped too rapidly, the potential movement blur one into another…

(3) You can further note that the tempo, rate of flip, is dependent upon the number of pictures involved in the production of each movement— too few pictures (with too great a jump between each extension of the lines of movement pic. to pic.) require a slow flip page to page… and too many pictures (with too little extension of lines of movement) require fast flipping for a move to be mentionable at all.

If you prefer this thumb-in-hand method of motion picture making, take your pick, your paper-pics, and be off; but as the movable picturing obtained by this method is not easily projectionable, I'm returning my considerations to the strip of celluloid and moving picture machinery.

(I)

The flippist part, of the above mentioned process (in the moving picture projector, and in some viewers) is called: *the shutter.* It is (in most projectors) a thin piece of metal cut approximately to a half-circle (cut so it looks like a metal pie almost half-eaten). It is located in the machine somewhere between the light source (the place where the light from the bulb is most concentrated by a condenser lens) and the place where the film strip passes, called *the gate.* The shutter whirls around a number of times a second, allowing light to pass thru a single frame of the strip of film in place at a rectangular window in the gate called *the shutter opening* (when the cutout, or eaten part of the pie, is passing) and then blocking all light (when the metal, uneaten piece, is having its revolution past the shutter opening). The actual picture-mover is of course not a thumb but a relatedly named instrument called: *the claw*. This is a movable metal part which, when the machine is in operation, jerks out beside the top of the shutter opening, and disappears at the bottom only to appear again at the top to repeat the process a number of times a second. When a film strip is loaded in the gate (that is, between the two plates of smooth metal designed for film passage) the claw will engage with each sprocket hole on the outside edge of the film, pull the strip down a frame at a time, and repeat this process with regularity for the length of the film. It essentially controls the stop-and-start movements of the strip of film, but its actions are dependent upon two wheels, one on each side of the gate, whose outer edges are spoked by a number of little claws which, during revolution of the wheels, convert the continuous unrolling and rolling-up movement of the film into a stop-start movement for precise control by the claw in the gate. These wheels, so crucial to moving pictures, have remained essentially unnamed, but I call them: *sprocket-wheels,* bless them. Where you have a continuous movement converted into a discontinuous, stop-and-start, movement and back again, you need two areas of slack in a strip of film. When threading a strip of film into a projector, leave a loop on either side of the gate, between the gate and the sprocket-wheels, for this purpose.

(2)

The timing of the flipping, flip-rhythm, is dependent upon interaction between the shutter, the claw, and the sprocket-wheels. The shutter and the claw are synchronized so that the shutter is only open when the claw is disengaged from the sprocket hole and the frame is held perfectly still in the gate, so that the light passing thru the shutter opening and the film frame projects only one picture, held absolutely still, at a time, and not the movement of the strip of film. When the shutter closes, cutting off all light, the claw engages the next sprocket-hole and moves the film strip down one frame and disengages again before the next revolution of the shutter allows light to pass. The sprocket wheels, on either side of this process, keep unraveling and rolling up the film in time to the shuffle of the claw and the whirl of the shutter, insuring space enough of top and bottom loop for the stop-start dance of the film thru the gate.

(3)

Flip-tempo, the speed with which a film strip passes thru the gate, is determined by the speed of the motor controlling all synchronous movements; and (in most projectors but only a very few kinds of viewers) this speed can be set at either 16 frames per second, called: *silent speed*; or 24 frames per second, called: *sound speed*. (Some silent projectors run only at 16 frames per second, and a few silent projectors run at a variety of speeds which are essentially undeterminable—the latter being also true of most viewers, which have no motor and are dependent upon the speed with which the film is pulled thru by hand, but a few, very expensive, viewers are motor driven and are both variable as to speed and also able to run at silent and sound speeds.) The determination of proper speed is dependent upon the film strip. For instance, if there is a great leap between each movement of your incoming wave, you will find the illusion of continuous movement, and speed of movement more believable if the film strip is projected at 16 (or even less) frames per second. If you have taken a long time, and many frames, to draw your wave in, then 24 (or even more) frames per second may be required to speed your movement up to believability. Naturally, this is also a question of taste, a determination of style, and ultimately an altogether individual matter which I leave up to you.

[(Viewers are also called *editors;* and, as that name implies, they are principally used while editing film strips into a larger continuity. As they do not project the image across much space (and are essentially for identification purposes rather than show) they approximate the motion picture effect much more simply, and less effectively, than the projector. The film is threaded between two metal plates, *the viewer gate,* but usually engages only with one sprocketed wheel, on either side of the gate, which completely replaces the claw of the projector. No loop is needed because *the claw wheel,* as I call this viewer wheel, turns a cylinder (under a window in the viewer gate) which contains a prism that scans the frame of the film strip (as it continuously moves) in a way which gives each frame the appearance of remaining still (while light is passing thru) and reflects these seeming-still pictures thru a series of internal mirrors and onto a frosted glass called: *the viewing plate.* Thus the film strip passes, from left to right or vice versa, emulsion side down or up, depending on the kind of viewer, in as straight a line as possible thru a gate and over, or under, a clawed wheel. Motor controlled viewers, usually called: *Movieolas:* thread much the same as a projector.)]

If you are more inclined to *take* machines for granted, and have thus *given* very little attention to the foregoing, admittedly difficult, description—I offer the following simple, push-button, instructions to permit you to thread your film by rote, by hook or by crook, or whatever:

(1) Place the emulsion side down, usually.
(2) Engage outer sprocket holes with the spokes of the upper sprocket wheel.
(3) Make a small loop above the polished metal plates.
(4) Slip the film, emulsion side out, usually, between the two polished metal plates, or into what is called the gate.
(5) Make sure your film is in position where the little claw

beside the window on the inner gate plate will be able to engage with your sprocket holes.

(6) Find the lever which presses the outer gate firmly against the inner gate.

(7) Make a small loop under the gate.

(8) Thread your film around the sprocket wheel under the gate.

(9) Find the shortest route around whatever wheels are left to get the head end of your film onto the reel for wind ing it up.

PART TWO : ON SPLICING

Dear Gregory:

Your letter affords me the opportunity to go into some details of film technique which might be of use to many filmmakers; so I'm making a carbon of this letter to send to The Co-Op—heaven knows I dislike writing about technique (I mean, it is so much more exciting to allow the lettering mind to explore imagi-nation, aesthetically adventure, et cetera); but as many a mountain climber has perished for lack of skill with a pick-axe, tangled himself in his own rope, and so un-forth, many creations are still-born out of technical inadequacy. I am *not,* heaven also knows, referring to any of your work; for you have always mastered whatever techniques were needed to fulfill your creative needs—it is because you will make good use of whatever information I send you that I am thus herein moved to detailing techniques which *might* be of more general use also. I have long felt there ought to be at least a section of *Film Culture* devoted to exchange of technical information between filmmakers. While this might prove dull reading for the purely audience readers of that magazine, it oughtn't: for I have discovered it impossible to communicate certain aesthetic information to technically ignorant audiences, have found it like trying to explain a pun to a child who doesn't even know the same sound can have several meanings, have felt audience frustration similar to the frustration I had when forced to attend a football game at Dartmouth and expected to cheer or groan at certain intricacies of the game which remain obscure to me to this day because I never learned the rules: for there is a vast area of any art where the grammar of that art and its technique are interrelated and even synonymous (in the sense of: to be taken for granted); and one of the definitions of any medium could, and perhaps best *ought*, to be in terms of the technical limitations of that medium —a great deal of wishing-washiness would be drained from aesthetic criticism were such an *actual* taking-measure of the medium prerequisite to any pie-eye-in-the-skyisms.... I mean, at least a critic *ought* to carry the standards he refers to for every put-down of a creator as heavily as if he were bearing a very real flag in a windstorm.

I encounter very few problems intercutting color and black & white. I always shoot, and (as I too edit original film) use in editing, reversal film—unless I want a negative image as the final screen image...and/or unless I might happen to be shooting color negative to be making positive prints therefrom. I assume what's worrying you is whether or not color and black & white film bases will splice together; and I would like to pass along certain splicing tips I learned the hard way (and hope you'll reciprocate). To begin with I always use double-perf film, if possible, in photographing. This always permits a four-fold use of any strip in relation to any other strip in editing for greater flexible handling of any (particularly abstract) image in movement, albeit the two uses of that strip of film (that is: when turned over or base-up, as its called) will soften the image slightly in printing (as the focusing devise in the printer is set on assumption that the emulsion side of the film is consistent throughout). Many times, in editing, then I'm forced to make a base-to-base splice—this is actually, if well made, a stronger splice than the regular emulsion-to-base splice. Now, as you know, in the usual splice the emulsion is scraped off one of the overlapping bits of film to be spliced because the cement will not weld any but base material; so, theoretically, one wouldn't have to scrape in a base-to-base splice at all; but I find it advisable *always* to "rough-up" the base side to be spliced, even in regular splicing. In emulsion-to-base splicing I put a small dab of cement on the base piece and immediately wipe it off, then lay down cement on the scraped emulsion side and weld the two. In a base-to-base splice I scrape one of the bases just the same, with perhaps less scraping, as if it were emulsion—then proceed as usual with the other base side. I arrived at this procedure out of the necessity of splicing many different kinds of film—for instance, certain different kinds of black & white film go together very difficultly and there is a bluish base B&W film which won't splice well *at all* unless its base is "roughened-up" with either cement or scraping. For these reasons I am also drawn to use scrapers which roughen film unevenly while scraping—find a fine grain strip of emery-paper (not board or cloth) best in this respect. Base-to-base splices also leave an often noticeable bar of dark across one of the images (of double emulsion, so I often turn the film over after splicing and meticulously scrape off the emulsion of the intruding picture. This brings up the problem of the noticeability of the splice in 16 (& 8) mm. The commercially professional way to make the splice invisible is the one I'd guess you usually use, that is: "A&Bing" as it's called where two synchronous rolls of film are created with black leader always on one roll & picture on the other, splice always tucked under black leader, pictures overlapping only where a dissolve from one to another is wanted or where the two are to be superimposed... but I have found this method altogether too distracting while creatively editing original and, of late, I usually have multiple superimpositions going on AB,

The Wonder Ring

ABC, and even (in Part 4 of *Dog Star Man*) ABCD rolls with no room left on the synchronizer for splice-hiding rolls even if I wanted it. During Part 1 of *Dog Star Man* I became particularly concerned that the splice SHOULD show (as a kind of aesthetic counterpoint to the plastic splicing and the fade-out-fade-in, etc.... The Splice, that black bar breaking two kinds of white, operating aesthetically as a kind of kickback, or kick spectator out of escapist wrap-up, or reminder ((as are flares, scratches, etc. in my films)) of the artifice, the art, et set-TO) and I became very involved in the splice-bars as operative visual cramps upon, for instance, the baby's face in Part 2 of *Dog Star Man*...and you can imagine (apropos my comments on page one of this letter) my difficulty in explaining how splice-bars compress that face and then break-up into the hand-drawn lines struggling for verticals to an audience which, for the most part, doesn't SEE splices, even in a white field, or have the vaguest notion how individual moving pictures are put together. Of course, aesthetic involvement WITH the splice does increase the need to be able to hide the splice when it isn't wanted (as it mostly isn't in Part 4); and the best technique for *that*, aside from A&B rolling, is the use of splicing tape, so that the cut can be hid exactly between frames; BUT, to the sensitive eye, the splicing tape lays down a wavery pattern particularly noticeable on white fields where there is usually the *most* concern for hiding the splice. Kenneth Anger told me he used this transparent tape exclusively on *Scorpio Rising* and that, by prearrangement with the laboratory, he only had to use it on the emulsion side, thus decreasing tape-glue image by half. Next best for hiding splices is The Negative Splicer (so named because it's used almost exclusively when splicing negative film because all splices thereon will turn out very noticeable white bars when positive print is made) and this makes a very much narrower splice but one which also requires much more care & ability for it to hold in printing. Every time I go to make a splice regularly I decide which of the two joining frames will carry the splice bar. If I want to semi-hide it, I'll usually choose the darkest and/or most complex image; but very often a lighter but more rapidly moving image will hide the bar better and/or an image mainly composed of horizontals, etc., etc., etc. Sometimes, for instance, I choose to leave the double emulsion bar in a base-to-base splice because it cuts off part of the preceding image and makes a plastic flow into the following image, etc., etc., etc. Sometimes in cutting B&W to color the partial super-imposition of overlapping emulsions creates a one-frame transition of aesthetic smoothness, et cetera...and, in other words, all these etceteras stand for one whale of an aesthetic involvement in The Splice. Even splicing cement doesn't just mean to me "that which holds two pieces of film together"—I know it's a solvent which welds film and this knowledge has led to its use in chemical treatment of film-that is, I've dissolved images, "painted" with it, mixed it with paints and clorox and salt and lacquers, etceteras. I found, for instance, that the glue of splicing tape crystallizes into certain recurring patterns when heated (with an iron) to certain temperatures (which I can only specify to the extent of "low" "medium" and "hot" on the average iron as corresponding respectively to "large, overlapping 16mm frame in most cases, unwieldy aggregates with large center & fine snow-crystal points," "clusters attached to each other," and "even textured small crystals in a field." *Mothlight* was made without recourse to heating; but *Dog Star Man* Part 2 involves the packing of material (even mica, which raised temperatures and scattered crystals like explosive material from it) & punched-out pieces of film packed between a *very* thin clear leader & splicing tape, all packed also with chemicals, Elmer's Glue, Nu-Skin, etc., depending on the piece, and (in most cases) heated with an iron welding all into a predetermined crystalline pattern. (It should be mentioned, for the record here, that I had no less trouble getting Part 2 printed than I did with *Mothlight*. *Mothlight* original, packed between splicing tape, was too flexible for the printer. Part 2, using thinnest leader available & tape, was too INflexible…part of this problem being mica shavings & the stiffness created by crystallized glues. There is also one hell of a problem getting splicing tape to lay down evenly onto clear leader, a less-flexible material, for any length—I'm next going to try exclusively filmy glues (like Nu-Skin) and cut up the splicing tape every foot or so, *that* the sprocket holes can be realigned at center of every second-and-a-half of film. Well, I see I've diverged a bit from The Splice; but I sense it's a divergence which may save you some time and repeated effort—as P. Adams told me you might be using film collage techniques in your *Illiac Passion*…and PLEASE send me any information you gain from working with these techniques—names of glues, for instance, would probably be worth thousands of words of aesthetics to me.

Now I sense the desire to close off *this* letter and hedge on the major question of *yours* because I cannot offer much encouragement regarding your current felt-needs of two-size screen simultaneity in projecting *The Illiac Passion;* AND YET I DON'T WANT TO DISCOURAGE YOU FROM ATTEMPTING ANYTHING, no matter how impossible-seeming, WHICH MIGHT PERMIT YOUR MUSES TO SHOW US ALL *SOMETHING NEW,* even if utterly other than what *you* think *you* want to be showing. So then, the following is simply to give you an idea what you're up against. For the rest: FOLLOW YOUR A MUSE MEANTS…okay? As you already know, unless you can get your entire vision onto one strip of film (no matter how many separate and separately framed images thereon) you run into almost impossible problems of distribution, etc. I think you're right to feel that THIS shouldn't stop you if your feeling of necessity urges you into a technically difficult area, particularly if the technical difficulties are only reflections of fulfillable lacks in distribution (after all, you and I made films for years when there wasn't really anyone to distribute or much of any audience to distribute TO)—BUT there are limits to this consideration… If I make a collage film which can't be printed or projected at all, then it is, after all, more of a necklace or wall decoration than a film. Kenneth Anger's *Inauguration of The Pleasure Dome* was finally edited into a triptych version (one large center screen, two small screens winging either side) requiring 3 synchronized projectors (and 3 screens) for screening. I worked constantly with Kenneth for a couple days in Brussels in 1958 attempting to bring this triptych screening off. All projectors came out of sync during all rehearsals & the public screening. Finally 3, out of the 7 judges, agreed to give up their lunch hour one day for a final try—which succeeded. There were about 15 people who saw this performance. These are the only fifteen, to my knowledge, who have ever seen the completed version of *Inauguration of the Pleasure Dome*. The experience was so incredibly beautiful that I would never for a moment consider the single track as more than a teaser of the total experience   NO MATTER *WHAT* THE PROJECTOR PROBLEMS OF THE LATTER, all of which I'm *very,* painfully, aware of from the experience...Okay? At Brussels, 1958, there was also a 7-synchronized-projection (involving 7 differently shaped screens) as a semi-constant attraction in The Polish (I believe?) Pavilion. The film they showed was a so-so travelogue; but the technique was fascinating—for instance, a dancer would leap from one screen, cross another, and land on a third, while four others were flashing scenes of audience, other dancers, orchestra, etc...there being a real attempt to keep sense of integrality. Kenneth and I were particularly intrigued to find out how it all worked; and we were not too surprised to find an electronic computer was operating all 7 projectors on a stop-start basis, a vast room of equipment constantly supervised by several german-types rushing from one computer component to another and cursing constantly, apologizing for everything being "out-of-sync." My point is that synchronism (which is here synonymous with aesthetic perfection) is dependent upon getting the experience onto one track, one strip of film, WHICH COULD ACTUALLY HAVE BEEN DONE, by either Kenneth or The Polish Govt., BY PHOTOGRAPHING ALL IMAGES THRU MASKS IN THE APERTURE and/or, if money enough, BY HAVING FILM MASKED IN THE PRINTING STAGES, using the usual superimposition techniques, but so masked that no image ever superimposes on another. But, dear Gregory, it doesn't sound to me as if you could afford to so treat the material you've already shot and/or reshoot material using said masks. I don't know just where, from your letter, you want to put your larger picture in relation to your smaller; but when we saw Harry Smith's *Marvelous* film at the Co-Op, Allen Ginsberg told us that he, when showing the film, would project slide images around his frame—and I remember thinking how expensive it would be just to get this simple device transferred onto single strip of film: it would involve shooting the slide image (masked accurate in center) into 35mm film, then A&Bing the two together & making a final composite print, the expenses being in accurate masking of the external to internal image, even tho', in his case, it wouldn't have to be too accurate as all his images occur in a black field, so that the shape of the image makes its own variable screen...something I've been working on in Part 4: *Dog Star Man* by laboriously painting out, a frame at a time, all but the image desired—and the painting can never be perfect enough to avoid a wavering edge which, thus, I extend into expression, viz: my masking becomes black sky breaking into stars, multicolored patterns (closed-eye visions) and scratched out shapes and objects (re-call visions). There is a masking tape you could block out some areas of your frames with; but you could never lay it down carefully enough to avoid a wavering line which would also be constantly fluttering with the irregularities of spilled under glue—a dynamic visual which would constantly pull the eye away from the photographic images to its vibrant edge. No, effective masking really has to be done in the shooting stage unless you're after effects similar to

hand-painting or unless you can afford the expenses of laboratory optical effects which can only be achieved by step-print-
ing (frame-at-a-time printing)...which would be the staggering
expense of Harry Smith's film—because, you see, he would
have to have his central images (the only ones I saw) reduced in
size to leave room for the surrounding images on the frame, or
else get some laboratory to retool for one-to-one printing of
16mm image in center of 35mm frame, then superimpose this
onto 35mm shots of his slide images...then, as you know, re-
duce the whole thing to 16mm for distribution.

Well, I hope all of this has been of some help to you; and I
very selfishly hope you'll reciprocate with technical information
of your own, particularly if you get involved in masking during
the shooting stages...I am very definitely being drawn into the
area of multiple imagery and image shapes within the field of
the frame (have, for instance, punched and/or cut holes in black
leader and dropped images into isolated black spaces in Part 2—
a **MORE** laborious activity than hand painting) and am much
inspired by Harry Smith's work, which I hope you'll get a
chance to look at.

PART THREE : MAKING LIGHT OF NATURE OF LIGHT

"Any fool can see for himself—," like they say...
It is the light we share.
I had meant, since beginning "The Moving Picture Giving
and Taking Book," to write about the taking of light, the use *of*
it: taking a light reading, so to speak—*with* a light meter, as it's
called ... *for* the figuring out, like they say, the where-abouts, on
the movable ring of the lens marked with "f," the numbers of it
should be placed so that a picture may be taken. As I came to
worry the subject in my mind's eye, came to see where I'd left
off writing this book altogether and to foresee how impossible it

was becoming to write what was left of it, I finally arrived at the
thought that the book had perhaps better be called: "The Moving Picture Giving Book" and that I had better let it go at that.
In that light then, if you'll pardon the pun/fun of it, I've come
to the beginning of wanting to *make light* of all of taking—of
light, of *pictures,* of *others,* of *myself* in this "take," as an "exposure before development" is called, this taken then of my mind's
eye moving thru thought to language in this writing.

My first instruction, then: if you happen to have a light
meter-give it away…otherwise: give over reading this further and
get on with the game of numbers you're playing and its absolute
sets of what is *scene:* for I am going on, from here, with *seeing*—
any/everyone's ultimate gift to the motion picture medium.

Beg, borrow, or buy (I do not believe in stealing) a moving
picture camera with at least one lens on it (a "used" 8mm camera is perhaps most in need of your blessings and will, thus, very
likely come to you easily in the family attic or for ten to fifteen
dollars *at most* from a store—but please don't accept a magazine
camera, even as more than temporary gift, as it will cost you
more money for film in the long run…and please NO "automatic exposure" photo-machine, either—that "seeing eye" dog
of a camera). Get a roll of film, *any* film that is the same millimeter as your camera. Somewhere on the box of it, or on a paper on the inside of it, or from the store proprietor, you will find
a number coming after the letters A.S.A.: and if your film is a
"color" one you will find the information as to whether it's a
"Daylight" or a "Tungsten." Keep all this information in mind.

Let us suppose to start with a "black & white" film, as that is
usually less expensive. Let us even suppose, to start to begin, that
you have not yet given yourself a camera. Collect yourself a
handful of tiny objects, such as would sit neatly on a fingernail,
and also an empty spool and film can the size and millimeter of
the full one you have in hand, and a small or "pencil" flashlight.
Find the darkest room available to you; and sit in it for awhile,

some ten to fifteen minutes say, looking all around for the light. You will find yourself, thus, fulfilling the initiation rites of many religious cults: but you need not let that worry you. Look for any light coming in under doors, thru curtains, or wheresoever; and cut it off with old rag stuffing, thick coats over windows, etc...and you need not worry about that, either, for, as you cut off the light you're *used* to, you will come to *be given* to see many kinds of light you may not have known existed before.

If you begin to feel foolish in this darkened room doing these things, please continue; but if you've only come to find the me-in-your-mind as foolish for the above writing, then please stop reading and try, rather, something on your own until you've managed to make a fool of yourself—for the writing, from here on out, is specifically for the "fool" who can "see for himself" ...no other than that in mind.

When the room is dark of all light you're used to, and before you begin to look for more light than may come to you, open the box and/or can of film and place it on the one side of you, with the empty reel and its can on the other side of you. Unwind some film (a good five feet or so). Attach the end of it to, and wind it up on, the empty reel (a piece of tape will help). Then place both reels in their cans, bending the film carefully over the edge of each can, so that the lids may be put on without more than gently folding the film, without more than a soft diagonal crease in the film, without tearing, etc. There should be, then, several feet of film between closed cans. Place this firmly on a flat surface (tape, again, will help) so that the sticky side (when moistened to test it between fingers) is up. Place your tiny objects along the length of the film. You may, of course, do this as carefully or as haphazardly as you choose. If you choose to give your care you will remember that each space between sprocket holes (which you can feel with your fingernails in the dark) is an individual picture which will when projected flash in some other darkness at a fraction of a second—the area between and to the direct side of any two sprocket holes in 8mm and "single-sprocket" 16mm, the area within the rectangle of any four sprocket holes in "double-sprocket" 16mm, the area to the side of any four sprocket holes of "single-sprocket" 35mm between the four on one side and four on the other of "double-sprocket" 35mm, etc. The more you think of these things while placing your objects on the film, even in the dark of your first endeavor, the more you give of form, of yourself thus to form, of the medium in the eventual projection of images, as always, about to be made.

Think of your flashlight, then, as a wand, for it is something more magic than a flash that we want of it, something more than any simple light, as we're used to, use of it. We want to make a ray—a Man Ray we'll call it, in honor of the man, so named, who first made it—directed by all of the thoughts, as above, and conditioned by two pieces of information kept in mind: the "A.S.A." number and, if color, the indication of "Daylight" or "Tungsten"...but, assuming again "black & white" film, let us assume a number after A.S.A. A small one, say between one and ten, will tell us that the film will take a lot of the light we give it to make an "exposure." A large number after A.S.A., say any number above fifty, will tell us that the film is very sensitive, so to speak, to light and will overexpose, as they call it, with the slightest bit of our illumination. Let us assume, to start then, an A.S.A. 5—the American Standard Association's average exposure rating for most motion picture "sound stock" film...this low rating will permit us a great deal more play of/and/with light in our giving exposure to the film. We can possibly even use the pencil flashlight to write directly upon the strip of film, if we write quickly and if the point of light of it is sharp enough, focused enough. As we move our wand away from the film, its beam spreads till, finally, evenly over the whole length of the strip, its exposure is interfered with only by the objects we've placed on it and their shadows. As we think of its beam as a ray, we may come to direct it elsewhere and only indirectly light the film; and as we come to think of the ray as a Man Ray each one can then, honoring tradition, become aware of what's undone and, being that self each is, direct the particular ray in hand, wave that wand wheresomever, as is most wanted, around whatever particular room in relation to the strip of film, writing directly upon it in one place and never permitting the light to shine other than indirectly upon it in another, creating a dance of the shadows of the objects placed upon it, throwing shadows of objects in the room across it, et cetera...but, whatever each chooses to do with this instant, *we* ALL *share* in this: *the light* can only illuminate that room for a very few seconds for the film's exposure, film's take, as it were. Even with an A.S.A. of 5, I would guess that more than two or three seconds of direct light, from however small and dim a flash wand, would expose the film to the extent that, when developed, it would be clear leader (if reversal film) or black leader (if negative film) as defined at the beginning of this book: and we would thus—for we all *do* share the light, share thus the conditions of time of light in relation to film—be back where we started from, with no trace upon the film, no sign or record even, of the magic each was making in the room of his or her most individual dark. The higher the A.S.A. number of the film the further must the wand be kept from the strip and/or the quicker the speed of illumination. But if all has gone well, each will have (when the film is developed) what is called "A Rayogram" for moving picture projection. But before developing, I would suggest that the process, as described above, be repeated for the entire length of the roll of film, each exposed strip being taken up into the can on the one side as the unexposed strips are unraveled from the other. As should be obvious, the whole length of film need not, indeed *should* not, be done all at once. Other than tiny objects may be placed upon the film, as say cloth for texture shadows, glass for refraction patterns, etc. And, assuming your film is color, various colored glasses or filters may be placed upon the strip, the point of the wand, or around the room, even, for a play of hues. If the film is a "Daylight" one, all whatever-colors will transform on film to completely other-colors because the film was exposed to flash wand rather than the sun wand intended—generally speaking, there will be more yellow in everything (unless it overexposes) because the flashlight will not be passing thru the blue of the sky as the sun's light does before exposing film...and you can, thus, put a "sky" in front of your wand in the form of a bluish filter taped onto your flashlight to render more approximate colors with "Daylight" film. If your film is marked "Tungsten," you'll know that word refers to the filaments of your flashbulb or electric-light-other and that the "sky" or blue of it has been put already into the film itself by the manufacturer, so that without you adding a filter the colors will be rendered more approximately—tho' in truth, they will still be transformed utterly into colors other than those of the objects placed upon the film, or between the light and the film, etc.: and I would hope you have the good sense to be aware of these differences when the film is developed, bless you.

Now if all the above does seem an end in itself, have patience for I, too, am tired of these mechanical limitations, would have us share more mysteriously in the light, am about to fool *with* the camera (rather than professionally fool it) and, for the sake of illumination become the fool *of* the camera and all its means (being amateur—lover...at heart). But if the above be beginning for you, quit reading and get on with it...joy to you!

Now, a camera can be thought of as a small closet (box) into which the film may be put (with pegs to hang the full and empty spools upon and a gate, much like the projector's described earlier, to thread the film thru) which has a wand-like light focuser (lens) screwed into it so that whatever external illumination which is "gathered," as it's called, by the wand *can* be focused into an image on the surface of the film, can *be,* thus, recorded by the light-sensitive grains of the emulsion of the film so as to be developed, later, into a picture which is projectionable. The motor of the camera simply conditions the movement of the film in relation to the shutter (the same as in the projector except that, in camera case, the film is always stilled for the ingathering of light, at shutter's opening, rather than for the projection thereof thru the film). When we hold the camera, therefore, we have the whole closet as well as wand in hand, stand IN the light and condition whatever of it and of images of objects reflecting that light we wish to affect the surface of the film. The motors of most cameras will permit us to flash light onto the strip of film at a variety of speeds by presetting a dial on the outside of the box which conditions and indicates how fast the film is moving thru the gate (usually marked: "8-12-16-24-32-48-64," etc.—meaning: "8 frames per second–12 frames per second," etc. because the speed with which the shutter opens and closes is conditioned by the number of times the film is stopped-and-started-etc. each second. We can also control the dimness and brightness of these flashes of light by setting the ring marked "f stops" around the lens itself (typically marked: "f 1.5-2-2.8 4-5.6-8-11-16-22"—meaning, for all intents and purposes, that when the lens is set at its lowest number, say "f 1.5," its iris, as it's called is *wide open,* like an eye in the dark; that at "f 2" it is a little bit closed, permitting less light; that at "f 11" it's about half closed; and that at "f 22 its almost closed, like the iris of an eye looking straight into the sun or at sun's direct reflection on a beach or bright snow scene) because, for *our* intents and purposes the "f stops" are like distances we keep between the flash light and the film according to the A.S.A. of it. If the A.S.A. is a low number, such as A.S.A. 5, then we can set our lens at a low "f," say "f 1.5," on a bright day even and still get an image upon it. If it is a high number A.S.A., such as "A.S.A 120," closing our lens to "f 22" may not suffice under the same circumstances to make other than white or black leader: but then these "circumstances" also depend, for picture, upon the speed of the film and, thus, shutter, and of course upon whether one is under the sun of this bright day or in the shade of it, in a house, etc. These many circumstances cause most photographers to use a light meter to determine their exposure, the setting of the "f stop" ring, etc.: but I suggest you play the fool, along with me, fool around in the light *with* your camera, be the fool *of* both (fool neither) and come along on an adventure, the nature of which is the nature of light itself.

First we must deal with the light *of* Nature, then with Nature of Light. And set your science aside, please, as we've no more use for it than what is *of* it as embodied in the camera in hand—an ordinarily closed system (as any machine) for taking pictures …which I am about to cause to flower (as my usual) wide openly in a gift of in-and-out-sight to the means of it. The camera will try to give back simply taken pictures (as that's what it's made for) but in the exchanges between us (myself and machine) there'll be, if I'm lucky as usual (and for you too if you're able as anyone), *a made thing* (an un-pic'ed image) which gives as much as it takes, *an illumination* (made as much *of* as *with* light) which should be a joy to see. I might, as I often have before, make a discovery (called "creation" most usually) and you, too, might, if you can but give your eyes to the medium (as any maker finally must) as a gift *beyond* any desire, to see or other, any re-quest, etc. "We shall see" refers to conditions, such as technical limitations, which we share, as we share the light. "I see" is an unconditional surrender to the light for a fool's vision. When giving sight to the medium, *"with, not through,* the eye" (William Blake*), *with,* rather than thru, machine, *with* any means at your bestowal (rather than disposal), *with* the light, and naturally then OF all these things also as in any gift, the term "moving picture giving" takes on a blessed (and necessary to me) dimension, viz.:

If you will, but listen (give your attention) to the camera motor (as you press its button—*never*, please, at speeds higher than 32 frames per second when there's no film in it, as that will often snap its spring) and you will *hear* some semblance of the speeds of film's run thru it...if you will, then, think of yourself as collector of light, thru wand of lens, for gift to film, you can then come to know yourself as conditioner of the light entering the magic box you hold in your hand—that you can slow or speed up the flashes of it, on the film's surface, by changing motor speed—that you can collect the most of light you stand in by turning the "f" ring to its lowest number, opening the iris of the lens widest, and/or can limit the power of the sun itself with each "stop down," as it's called, to the highest number. And if you can, then, but give yourself to the light around you (keeping *sense* of the above conditions on circumstances) till you are attracted to one area or another of the direct or reflected light (taking *a stance* in relation to your surroundings), you will be able, by a pointing of lens and a turning of its rings, to give some of your inner illumination to the surface of that film (give the song of your *sensing,* what you've seen AND thought of it, to the film's heard movement in the camera), viz-a-viz:

If you want the light you're sensing to take shape upon the surface of the film, to etch itself there in sharp lines of the edges of its reflecting forms, you will guess at the distance *from the film's surface* to most of the objects within the rectangular space of your looking (thru the "viewfinder") and will set the numbers of the "foot" ring of your lens (usually numbered from "1 ft." to "∞," a symbol standing presumptuously for "infinity") accordingly; whereas, if you want the light to affect the film's face more impressionistically, you can "soften the focus," like they say; and, therefore, if you want light's tones unenclosed in shapes, you can set close object's image in "infinity" or

---

*For when William Blake writes, "We are led to believe a lie/ When we see *with* not *through* the eye," he proclaims his possibilities as a great "still" photographer and, as such, of extreme opposite inclination from a moving picture maker.

obliterate landshapes and distant forms with a "1 ft." setting. Wherever you would interfere with the light, take account of shadows as exactly as if they were objects placed upon the film emulsion in a darkened room, as if a setting of the lens to the exact distance of the shadow were a placing of the object flat upon film surface, etc. A breath upon the lens will often add the Western eyes'ed sense of halo, or the mystic's aura, or a whole fog even. A drop of water, or some similar refractor placed before the lens, will split the beams of any direct light into the very lines tunneling out of it which must, once, have given Western man the idea that the sun was in harness, or reigned, and then caused him to later create a way of seeing called "Renaissance perspective" we take too much for granted; and a soft focussing of these lines will spread these lines to rays, as clouds or dust storms often scatter sun. And many things may be put before the lens to simulate something of mind's eye, thought's light, on film—if you use a "Tungsten" film in the daylight, for instance, an orangish filter will render the colors what we call "truer," just as a blue filter is used with"Daylight" film to put some sky into electrical illumination, etc...but all of these conditionings I've written above are a hatch of hindsight, a taking of light for some use or other—not much more of a gift to the medium than the taking of a picture. Not being a poet, I cannot write much other than "about," write out of some past endeavor, whereas a gift is always a present, so to speak...it will take some very creative you in the gift of reading this to make this writing more than a take. Permit me to illustrate, become the reader myself of the below, now, blank of page in seeing search of nature of light, viz-ability:

"blank" (as all words) interfering with my read of the texture of the paper, the shadow-blackened creases and spots impressed on the white field of it—"white" coming to mind to block any seeing of the yellow of the lamplight upon it, reflecting from off it, and as if lying heavily across the whole surface of it—"yellow" blanketing the mind's eye as if to cover up the sense of the blue, as it's collected in each shadow, like pools with deep purple centers, or flaring palely blue over the whole surface and almost flickering at page top nearest my window in instreaming daylight—"blue" (as "purple" and "black" and all earlier color words) finally giving way to eye's sight of an other-than electric yellow whirling within blue on page and sky out my window in some as-if struggle with blue, an eddying all thru the air of these environs, which I follow up the margin of the page I'm reading till blue takes shapes surrounded by yellows of skylight, but shapes that are almost invisible under apparently shifting folds of "Tungsten" yellow, each blue whirl taking general shape of ball with curved comet-like tail, all shapes blackened in focus of concentration on the page, tho' easily seen bluishly out my window, all tailed-spheres spiraling as if in the heat of liquid gold (these being Reich's "Orgones" in, say, C. S. Lewis's "yellow space"?)—"Orgones" taking away all sight-sense of the vision, "Reich's" taking the experiencing away from me, and "C. S. Lewis" as literary reference intellectualizing my seeing beyond any sense of it...thus, all within that last parent-thesis disperses the vision, making sense *of* what was a sensing (do not, please, permit me to do that to you, dear reader)—my sense of "reader," "dear" or otherwise, interfering utterly with my reading of this page, blocking me in a lock of attention to the inks of its letters...but then...but then, the type marks—they wink at me—not as letters but, rather, as surfaces rainbowed over: and as my eyes open to them, relax into softened focus, the prisming lines bubble open into streams of colors infinitely varied—"infinitely" (that presumptuous word again) tips me off and into a searching concentration wherein the black-born colors *tend* to arrange themselves as follows: oranges, blues, greens: and, thus: oranges in curved lines or circles, with yellow at inner or center and red at outer or perimeter; and blues in lines graded to purple one side or the other; and greens as a weave throughout—"throughout" checking my concentration, causing a spread of vision across the whole page until I see similar-to black-born prisming colors moving, according to the first *tendencies observed,* among the comet-blue shapes and molten folds-over-folds of electric-yellow and in shadow pools, concentrations of prism-blues tending to impress upon me large (several inch once) *always elongated* shapes, ingatherings of prism-oranges *always forming circularly,* and green weaves shaping fields of their predominance *always* as *irregularly curled* as vines—three underlined "always"es demonstrate to me that I'm about to make a science and/or a religion of this endeavor, damnit, about to really try to *convince* someone else (some "dear reader" of the imagination) of my own eye's sightings, make sights of them in sets of laws and dogmas to *convict* all other (in a "damn your eyes," as the saying goes)—forgive me...I tire, viz:

...goodbye again, dear reader—I'm off to work: to try to gather light this particularly, even if (as in the past) I can finally only paint some approximation of these minuscule occurrences upon the film's developed surface...for film is never hypoed by the lab, "fixed" as it's called, beyond a maker's giving—his adding to it, thru paints and chemicals and superimpositions in editing, his senses of the light as seen—until that maker himself becomes too long exposed to the light of any particular piece of film and, thus, ceases to see *it* any longer...then, and then only, might a work be called "finished." As I've ceased to read myself herein, then, and have other livelier things to do, permit me to make (not "the" but)

an end.

[1966]

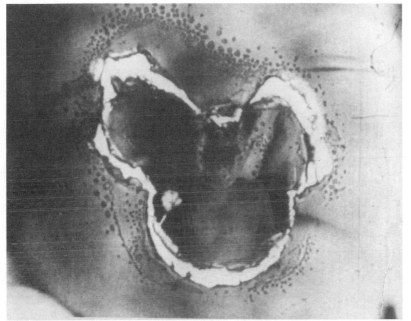

Dog Star Man

eight questions

H*ow do you finance films if not by a foundation?*
The first intimation I had that I was going to make a film
some fifteen years ago was when some friends and I were talking
about how sad it was that an artist couldn't work with the film
medium; that it was so prohibitively expensive that no artist
could work with it. I remembered that when I was a child I was
put in a boy's home called Harmony Hall—which was anything
but that-and forced to hold my hands above my head for two
hours because I had said to some other kid that anything was
possible, and he reported that I had said that you could cut off
somebody's head and that it would sprout wings and fly away.
And when that was thrown at me, when they said: "Is that possible too?" I said: "Yes, it's possible." So I was punished for having said this. And as I stood there, every time my hands touched
the wall they would hit them with a ruler. So I came at that time
to believe very strongly that anything was possible; I was either
going to be broken at that moment or believe what I had said. So
when my friend said that it was prohibitive for an artist to use
the medium, I didn't believe him. With that clarity that is real
presumption in the young, I said: "Well, I'm an artist and I'm
going to make a film." But that sounds too noble, because I was
terribly shy, and there was this girl that I wanted to go with, and
I was too shy to ask her straight out. So I cast her in the lead in
this film. Essentiaily, I began to make film in order to disprove
this statement and to make out with this girl.

And here's the financial side of it: we got some war-surplus
out-dated Dupont gun-camera film in fifty foot spools. And we
had to sit in the dark with pencils and unreel it onto spools and
make a splice in the dark so we could get hundred foot rolls.
And we then borrowed several cameras; also, we rented a camera for a couple of weekends. By the time, two years later, we got

a sound track on it, I suppose *Interim* had cost something like five hundred dollars. This is how I made that first film; it seemed to me too expensive.

The second film was sponsored: *Unglassed Windows Cast a Terrible Reflection.* It turned out to be something like a sponsored film. After that I began making my own films.

When I began my third film I had no money at all. I still wasn't convinced that I was a filmmaker. Like Jean Cocteau, I was a poet who also made films. That was how I thought of myself: I was Denver's Jean Cocteau. And this third film had been promised to the public: we had been trying to import Museum of Modern Art film classics into Denver, and we had promised the public three films, and couldn't afford to rent the third one. Someone had some outdated black and white footage and since it was cheaper to pay just the processing I shot the film to fulfill that third slot. It was a biting satire on what we used jokingly to call "desistentialism." Long before the Beats, this film (*Desistfilm*) prophesied the whole concept of the Beat generation. I used jokingly to say "We've got beyond the stage of existentialism, we've got to the stage of de-sistentialism." So I made this satire on that form of life which is destructive to the self. It had a sound track and cost something like a hundred and twenty dollars to an answer print.

So you see, each film comes in a different way. *Dog Star Man* (of which you'll see the *Prelude* tonight) was made while I had a job at a lab that agreed to process my film at cost while I was on the job. They never realized that I was to put through six thousand feet in two months' time. Also at this studio we had high speed cameras. So we had super equipment, and all that footage at a very minimal cost. And so it goes.

When I need to do something I somehow find the means to do it. And somehow, like magic, incredible coincidences occur that make it possible. Then all kinds of possibilities open. For instance, when some 16mm equipment was stolen, I had only enough money to buy 8mm equipment to replace it. So for three years now I've been making 8mm films I probably never would have made had it not been for this thief. For this I'm grateful: it's opened up a whole new area in my work.

Is your intent in making a film to communicate?

I get this question everywhere; and the big hangup is the word "communication." It's like this: let me explain by way of a story, a true story.

A man falls in love. The girl doesn't love him. She hurts him; she wants somebody to hurt and he wants somebody to hurt him, but he doesn't know that yet. He's downcast. Then he meets another girl and he loves her and she loves him. He no longer needs to try to communicate with her: they just take walks together, and make love, and talk. Then he has it: some expression of his love is out there in the world.

Then he takes her to introduce her to his parents, and he is involved in communicating again, and this is very difficult. Well, this is like when a man works out of love and the work is out there; and then he takes this work into society, and that's always very difficult. I mean no one truly understands it, just as no one's parents truly understand one's true love. Yet a work of art must have a life in society; once the artist has finished making it, it belongs to others. But he never made it with the idea of taking it into society. Any man that sets out to find a girl to introduce to his parents is never likely to fall in love. Any man that sets out to make a work for audiences is never going to make a work of art. A work of art is made for the most personal reasons—as an expression of love.

Could you tell us what you feel about 8mm?

First of all, it's cheaper than 16mm. Next—just picking up one of those little cameras relates me to the whole sense of amateur. It's an amateur medium. I have a growing conviction that something crucial to the development of the art of the film will come from amateur home-movie making, as well as from study of the classics: Eisenstein, Griffith, Méliès, and so forth. It's so small and lightweight-I stick it in my pocket, carry it everywhere—and so cheap: used 8mm cameras usually go for about fifteen dollars. Some, when they're used, are broken down and do extraordinary things, like failing to catch the film just right so it makes a particular pattern and flutter. One I had broke down utterly when I was doing an ocean film. Its spring broke permitting me to grind it at different speeds; so I would let the wave rush up very fast by grinding slowly, and then I'd suddenly zoom up so that the wave reached its peak in slow motion, and then I'd slow my hand down so that the wave would break up in an incredible order.

Then 8mm film is given such a blow-up on the screen that you can see the grain of the film stock much more clearly than in 16mm high speed film. The crystals that make blue look quite different from those making red and green. For years I've baked film, used high speed film and sprayed Clorox on it so as to bring out grain clusters. You might say it's inspired by impressionism, but it's a great deal more contemporary than that. I have been trying for years to bring out that quality of sight, of closed-eye vision. I see pictures in memory by the dots and moving patterns of closed-eye vision—those explosions you can see by rubbing your eyes, and even without rubbing; there's a whole world of moving patterns. It's a manifestation of the optic nerve, and God knows what else.

There are endless advantages to working with eight. Creative advantages. It's an entirely different medium from sixteen. It imposes a different kind of discipline because there isn't a way of easily working with A and B rolls and changing lights in the lab—some labs do it but it's pretty expensive. Editing, when there is editing, is on the order of the splice. Eight mm has freed me to work freely, much as an artist is freed in sketching.

If an angel were to give you money to work with 35mm, would you want to?

It doesn't work that way with me. To answer your question about an angel who would give me 35mm: usually it's the other fellow who gives us things like that. If you were to say: "We must have 35mm!"—poof, the telephone would ring and there he'd be, right out of Faust. For me, once, it did just that: I had been working on a lip-sync film. There I was with the dialogue on magnetic tape, and I had no equipment to do this, so there I was trying to iron the film, and it went "wreak-wrock," like this, and then trying to drop these accurately into the picture area where the lips (*mimes lip action*) (*Laughter*). Well, three hours of this and I'm out of my mind. Before I had a chance to cool off, the telephone rang. It was long distance and a voice on the other end said: "How would you like a million dollars worth of motion picture equipment to work with?" I should have hung up immediately or crossed myself or put some garlic on the phone (laughter) but like a fool I said, "Who is this?" As it turned out it was some guy who wanted something on his own who was pretending he could connect me with a college that actually had a million dollars worth of equipment and he claimed he could get me a job there. And we suffered for two months as a result of this phone call. Since then I've been very careful—you know, it's like the monkey's paw or Alladin's lamp: you get three wishes, yet no matter what you wish, it's stacked against you.

If I absolutely *had* to work in 35mm, I would simply find a way to do it. For instance, right now I need 35mm in my work in hand painting the image. I get 35mm film stock from the back of lab editing baskets, stock that would otherwise be thrown out. I've been working two years now and have three seconds done.

As I understand it, you feel that money and affluence are not a good climate for artistic endeavors?

It's a personal matter. Imagine Wallace Stevens as anything but a banker, the banker he was, moving in that world of dark shadows and thick rugs and mahogany staircases and rubber plants and semi-stained glass windows, moving down to the bank and its vaults and resounding echoes. All that's part of his milieu and he's incomprehensible without it. Some artists feel they need to move through this shadow world of the rich. It's very hard to talk about affluence and art because it's so much an individual matter. There's a kind of artist who will flourish and flower under a great cultural explosion, and Andy Warhol is an excellent example; and there are other artists who make a work that will not flower under that climate. Their art must be infinitely attended. The trouble with the cultural explosion is that it tends to engender a kind of interest in an art that can be viewed quickly, or a piece that can be viewed once, or a play that can be seen and comprehended once over television, or on the stage, or a paperback that you read once and then throw away or give to a friend. This may be exciting, but it is anti-art, as I understand it. I think one finally comes back to those things that are meaningful in one's life. Films are just beginning to provide this possibility where one can have them in their homes, in libraries where they can be come back to again and again in meaningful film viewings. I look forward to this very much, because it takes film off the stage, off the public occasion scene and out of the competitive arena. Such library facilities will provide for the necessity a viewer may feel to see a particular film. It's necessity that causes a work of art to come into being, and it is necessity that makes a viewer commit a work of visual art to memory. Such preservation constitutes the true continuity of culture.

I look at a work over and over, and then thoughts come. I think art is the expression of the internal physiology of the artist. It's that at scratch: the individual expression that can be attended by a person hearing himself sing and feeling his heart beat. And always it begins with and comes to this: a man attending his physiology and making an expression out of it. I think the first expression was some creature beating his chest to give out with the heartbeat, and then the feet danced, so the feet were expressing the heartbeat, and then the heartbeat was heard more complexly, and that made possible a greater variety of rhythms. Anyone who attends his own heartbeat can find the source of all rhythmic structures. And then there were pictures in the eyes. There was experience and there were memories and the memories came up and made a picture and there were things crucial to the picture, and they made of it a hieroglyph, and writing started there. And I think, at heart, that all art is today as it was then: man is supposed to be a million years old.

And the great artist is more aware of this, of these life cycles?
    I don't know. The great artist may be less aware of it. "Great" and "aware" are two words.

This would relate to the statement you made in a letter to Jonas Mekas: "Plant this seed deep in the underground. Let it draw nourishment from uprising of spirits channeled by gods."
    You know what this is like? It's like…this is strange because I kind of remember those words. Scientists tell me that short of the molecular structure in my brain there's not an atom left in me that wrote that, or very few. This is as if I presented you with a statement that you wrote eight, nine years ago. I don't know; I would say something different now. That sounds to me a little too rhetorical.

I'm intrigued though at the mention of the word "god" in connection with the earth. Was it chthonic deities you had in mind at that time?
    God knows, as they say, what I had in mind at that time. This afternoon we were talking, and the phrase came up, "the powers that be," how timorous people were about "the powers that be," powers which are, really—non-existent; powers which have so

dominated the American business world: powers which can be very beautifully defined as "the non-existent powers that be." And I said: "Take that to the nth power, and that's a power concept," but not *my* concept of god. My god is existence. My god is manifest in everything; not through power but through being, through an unfolding of being, through a willingness to dance with life and existence. All religions, however different, grant preeminently to man the power of the will. So that is my idea of "the powers that be"—the will of the dancer, open and willing, the will of the dancer.

[1967]

Scenes from Under Childhood

with love

There is no contemporary place for women in art, if art be considered a form in history the shape of which is determined by inventions which have shaped it and each invention of which answers the previous inventions which are crucial to it (as is clear in the medium of mathematics, etc.), because the form is male (as most historical forms are) and even overtly exclusive of woman (as even the subject matter of most, say, poems in the English language are premised thus—thus as content thus—thus as "form is never more than an extension of content" thus,—etc.) while yet each source of inspiration, creatrix of impulse throughout, is woman—the muse is female ...the beginning of any form is woman (as, say, contemporary medicine finds its roots in the natural activities of witches), as the first rite is rooted rightly in the imagination in a matriarchy. Each bull dike and each effeminate man extend bridges to and from, respectively, the world of the arts— these hang in space now, what*ever* the greatness of technicality which keeps them, those bridges, afloat (and you know what I mean when you temper this with the knowledge of, say, Gertrude Stein's *importance*) make side pockets on the trousers of historical art, that hierarchitectitiptitteploftical of man's doing, the UNdoing of which is always at the fly-open ("side pockets" makes me think of the story of Elizabeth Barrett Browning, more famous for her verse than her husband all the while she was living, breaking the rule they'd agreed upon: that they would not show each other's work to each other, working in separate rooms, hers the study directly above his, etc.: and coming down one day, coming up behind him as he was looking out the window, holding his head so he would not turn around, and slipping "Sonnets from the Portuguese" into his coat pocket, saying something like: "Read these later—if they do not please you, please destroy them," etc.)

...her coming to that most clear gesture as she became his wife, he her husband, came to understand the form of poetry thereby, and how the inability to see she might have created a new form, a woman's form, from scratch, so to speak, thus the loss of the old form, the knowledge of what she *never* had had, came possibly to kill her, caused the tragedy of her death in work at least despite both her fame *and* Robert's rightful awareness of the greater [than his] potential of her work, his continuous praise, etc. of the misleading terms of his praise, her room above [more removed from the earth] his, etc.). Ah, well...anyway, I see the possibilities of a woman's form or forms growing to a maturity, being a dress, bell open at bottom to all earth impulse, which answers at first to the needs of that sex woman is, and internally *her* organs, and becoming in time a form independent of male shape enough to permit each woman's invention to answer woman's invents in history *until* such time as male and female art may answer each other, via sex at first, I imagine, and furtively as in a lift of the skirt and some unzipping, but wherein the bridge is as extension of penis, as inspired at source, the opening of the form of woman as structured as her body, as sourced as her needs, and then, in time, as in love, the side-pockets will fall away, the hands of the masturbating man-shape of his medium be freed for embrace, their clothes in historical tatters from the workings of lust, be simply taken off and some art be reared in marriage, after all these poor bastards set adrift in the spaces of the imagination, some thus housed and finally homed, in love, growth of the union of these old arts inform them both thru its coming into maturity of their pasts, as do children always, for a being present of each in all. Okay, this is perhaps too metaphorical in my present writings here: but I sense this idea as center of beautiful possibilities, tho' it be only see/ metaphor in the moment..."see" for "seed" there encouraging me it is more real a sight in my imagination than I had imagined—must now hope to some time Freudslip "real" to "re all" and thus inform myself it is rooting solidly viz: spect to past.

[1967]

film:dance

Film is the oldest art of our time (in the sense Gertrude Stein finds America the oldest contemporary country).

Film as film is essentially undiscovered (in the sense D. H. Lawrence defines America undiscovered), and traditional aesthetics interfere with this discovery (essentially as Lawrence finds "democracy" impeding the discovery of America as America).

Film aesthetics take shape historically (as William Carlos Williams finds American history taking some European shape aesthetically).

Whereas:

Films shape themselves with reference to very much less sense of history and very much more reverence for history than any other possible art.

Films *take* shape most truly there from some immediate sense of presence.

Film *as* film shapes itself most usually in The Present *as* Gift.

Film is, thus, premised on physiological sense—*takes* Sense as Muse...is oldest art to center itself on that source of inspiration.

The technological means of moving pictures come into being to satisfy the need of (particularly Western) Man for an immediately (moving) permanent (picture) impress-extensability of (visual) sense.

The art of this is, simply, the making of these means full.

The art of this, complexly, is as and according to the needs of the man making.

The art of this, historically, is the individual's impress-extense of himself to the historical forms of art.

That is a chance.

It, as all chance, is physiologically centered.

It is, as un-rehearsed dance, determined by the immediately-present *sense*-ability of the individual dancer.

Film, as this dance, is particularly American:

Its central fact is space (as Charles Olson finds: "Space to be the central fact to man born in America");

Its permital abstract is pure energy (as Buckminster Fuller defines "efficiency," American-wise, as: "ephemeralizing *toward* pure energy").

Its internal limitation is individual physiology—lack of touch, sense-thereof/with geography...lack of ground—for energy, lack of direction, sense-ability-thereof/for geometry... lack of attitude—in space, (or as Gertrude Stein refines American definitions: "when they make the boundary of a State they have to make it with a straight line," contrary to European boundaries, *and:* "A sky is a thing seen when you look up, when you look up in America you see up. That is all.")

When, as mythed, Méliès made the first film splice, he created the possibility of a mind's eye art—its momentum subject to the dance of the intellect—its outer limitation the optic nerve endings of any individual.

As the splice became generally accepted, the motion picture medium ceased to be a flattened box stage of light into which something could be put—it became sight's gesture...the eyes had it.

American necessity, culminating in the genius of D. W. Griffith, gave it time/shape for memory's articulation—an optic nerve-end feed-back formality...the mind's eye's sway over any input.

As the Griffith grammar became generally accepted, the motion picture ceased to need to continue itself by classic cause-and-effect laws—it became sight's self searcher physio-logical.

Human animal necessity now moves most individually new world over to fulfill these means forth with more than gesture and never (the) less than search.

This is a dance.

As a dance, it is: as the body moves, the eye moves with it...
as the eye moves, the body is in movement.

But the dance, at worst, is premised pre-Méliès and, at best,
has come along a line of internal physiological self-awareness
only to sense of gesture.

The cine-dance, thus, is at worst an attempt of one medium
to put itself into another medium which will not meaningfully
be put upon. At best, it is a gesture art lacking grammar.

(An *almost* exception: Maya Deren, in *Choreography for Camera,* kicks casual-effectuals out in the edit of backgrounds, making them cinematic in-scapes, time-and-otherwise, but left the
dance in-classic-tact.)

(An almost traditional *sort of* outgrowth: others, most notably Shirley Clarke and Ed Emshwiller, have followed Deren's suit
and followed it up to various reactions of dancers *to* cinematic
shift-of-scene, superimpositions, etc.: but these are of technical
necessity, *re*-acts, even re-en-actments, of no more immediate
necessity than any seen-scene's accommodation of a dancer—
no more than through-true to cinema's dance...no more necessarily, centered on filmmaker's sense of seeing shaped by
memory's eye.)

But the Dance is as one, *any*one, exercises one's body, any
part thereof, at large (Robert Duncan says he writes poetry: "To
exercise my faculties at large").

And the Art of Dance is as someone is able to, and does,
extend himself, thus, through all his means to the World of
Dancing.

Cine-dance, truly, would seem to me to occur only as those
"means" might, of necessity, include a camera in dancer's
hand—(and it should be noted that both Deren and Clarke *were*
dancers before coming to film...and that Emshwiller, like Sidney
Peterson, another significant dance-filmmaker, is married to a
dancer—approaches the form, thus, through personal necessity).

But cinematic dancing might be said to occur as any filmmaker is moved to include his whole physiological awareness in any film movement—the movement of any part of *his* body in the film making...the movement of his eyes.

I practice every conceivable body movement with camera-in-hand almost every day. I do *not* do this in order to formalize the motions of moving picture taking *but rather* to explore the possibilities of exercise, to awaken my senses, and to prepare my muscles and joints with the weight of the camera and the necessary postures of holding it so that I can carry that weight in the balance of these postures through my physiological *re*action during picture taking and *to* some meaningful *act* of edit. I would like to think I share something of some-such with dancers: and I do, of course, simply...but rather more complexly, I find that this Art of Dance, its premise in physiology most historically (of all arts) granted, has taken itself too fore-granted.

Dance sits with all other "three dimensional arts"—Drama/ Sculpture/Architecture—having one hell of a time getting off the stage...it, like Drama, has forgotten its "continuity self" or else the "dis" any contemporary sense of "Space/ Time" kicks "Cause/Effect" with.

(An *almost* exception: "Events/Happenings"—but they, like "Op/Pop" depend/locate on audience, ergo *re*-act, and make gesture *out,* ergo premise themselves outside individual physiology...take an *imagined* sense as Muse, tend to woo it through to audience.)

I do not believe the "3-D" arts have taken all the possible contemporary means and/or found them in any individual hand.

I do not think there is, as of now, any cine-dance worth mentioning as such.

I *do* imagine that there might some day, through some dancer's necessity, be something of some-such: and I imagine the means of cinematography will be as simply taken as music now is and that the work of the dancer will, therefore, simply be called: Dance.

[1967]

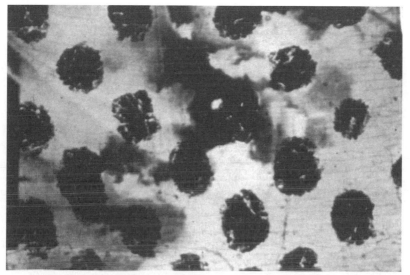

23rd Psalm Branch

the stars are beautiful

1) There's a wall there, a great dark wall with holes in it; and behind the wall is an enormous fire of white flame.

2) The stars are entirely in the eyes of those who look at the sky. If no one is looking at the sky, it is utterly dark. But the stars in the eyes are very much the same in all eyes; and those looking at the sky at the same time are all participating in the kinds of communication that have to do with stars.

3) It's a great roof studded with sequins. The movement of the stars is in relationship to the movement of the sun, giving the impression that the stars are moving across the sky.

4) The stars are optical nerve endings of the eye which the universe is.

5) Sparks from a train of God's thought.

> (I have one big toe in bronze and the other in eternity.)

6) There is such an intense brightness that we can't really see it. The sky is really burning white and the stars are black. The daytime is less bright and therefore the yellow, that is really there in daytime, we see as blue. The sun we see as yellow: It's really blue-black. *That* that we see as blue sky is burning away the black spot of the sun; and the sky at night is burning away at the black stars.

> (Novalis has seen the sun as black, and so has everyone who has closed his or her eyes on it. Retention colors are the only true colors.)

7) The stars are sparks from lightning.

8) The stars are the loopholes into 256 dimensions.

9) The fact is, the earth is falling into a well. The sun is the top of the well, the blue sky the walls. The stars are reflections of the real stars behind the sun.

10) It is a furry animal. The stars are silver hairs.

11) The sky is a cylinder to the moon.

12) The sky is all together, not composed in such great distances as we suppose. In truth, it is an old fire. The stars are small sparks, the sun a burning coal. The black of the sky at night is ashes, the moon a bubbling drop of water. This is the same with us, i.e.: as the universe burns, so do we. Our heads contain water very much like the sky holds moons. The burning in us keeps the water in our heads boiling and sputtering.

13) The sky is the dead decaying body of God; the stars are glittering maggots.

14) It is the back of a blue dragon; and we are the eye of the dragon, watching him die. The sun is the blood-hole.

15) The sky is a cup of tea which the earth drinks every day, then at night inverts the cup to read the leaves.

16) The sky is a lens of air magnifying a single atom of itself.

17) [There was one of these stories that I liked but didn't believe; so neither Jane nor I could remember it.]

18) [This one's fairly traditional]: The sun is the ejaculation of the penis in the vagina of the universe. The stars are the sperm searching for the eggs of moons.

19) The universe is part of a vast brain, the stars the firing of brain cells—each a visualization of the bark of a dog, i.e.: when a dog barks, the response in the ear of the sky is a star; when a dog howls, the response is the moon. The sun is where everything else goes to a further place or places; and we really don't know what happens there.

20) The stars are trembling silver strings to everyone's brains. The sun and moon are the eyes of the great puppeteer... Once a month he smiles and winks: He has control of our fates.

21) The day-sky is a pool of all our tears: the world is getting smaller and smaller. The night-sky is a blotter to all our black thoughts: there is very little space left.

22) The sky is the low-water beach on which are left phos-

phorescent plankton which will grow to be enormous beasts.

23) Light is everywhere; and the sky draws everything to it that we make. For instance, it draws our air and condenses it,'till it becomes black with our breathing; and it draws water in gigantic drops, which we see as stars. It draws the earth in streams 'till it blazes golden; and finally it draws all our fire into the ash of the moon.

24) The earth is a pool of brown watery waves in a forest of trees we see as stars near a golden bird flying after its white mate.

25) The stars are clear sounds; the sun a magnificent silence; the moon?…whispers that are almost sounds in the undulating wave of noise the universe is.

26) The sky is the solid state of time; the sun?…its emergence; the moon, the tube it all falls into. The stars are the fragments that never move on.

27) God, taking pity on those who stop smoking, made the stars to look like so many cigarettes burning, the clouds to look like smoke, the sun to remind them of the striking of a match, and the moon in the shape of a filter tip.

28) The night sky is a fold-over-pattern of the sun. The moon is a visual echo.

29) The stars are a flock of hummingbirds. If you look closely, you can see their wings flickering. The sun and moon are their flowers.

30) The sun, moon, and stars are the footprints of God (we are his head) as he walks currently in a circle.

31) Everything's happening at once; but the sky is a clock and makes it look like things are happening one at a time.

32) The stars and the moon are reflections of the sun which can't be seen.

33) Once upon a time, long long ago there was in the sky at night only the moon—as even now in the day there is only the sun. Then some wise men projected into the night sky hieroglyphs of their thoughts so that everyone who looked, af-

ter that, would know those thoughts and be wise also.

34) The stars are the places where snowflakes are made; each star has a different shape and makes a different shaped snowflake. When the snowflakes fall from the stars, they shrink and become changed in shape; and thus every snowflake also is a different shape.

35) The stars are the broken fragments of the mirror that reflects reality.

36) Big dust motes.

37) The nets are boiling.

Narrative script circa 1967
(as transcribed by Jane Brakhage,
night after night of their telling).

angels

       . . . move thru the qualities of shadow in a dif-
fraction of the light—the doors of illumination/home of angelical forces (as George MacDonald would have it: "...home
...is the only place where you can go out and in.")...
...and the shadows of shadows are the shadows of angels...
...and the fixed instants of constantly changing shapes are the
pictures they take of themselves:

                a smoke pattern in the hearth's wall,
                a cloud held in the mind's eye,
                a face in tree leaves...

...all that we call psychological projections are the movies of
the angels—
   the home movies of angels are qualities of light held as if in
midair—
   any gathering of dust motes in the light records the passage
of angels:

          for they do itch in the lungs when the soul is troubled;
          and they scour the hideout of the soul's enclosure;
          and they seize the brain in the body's fitfulness:
          and we do sneeze them out—
          cough up whole angels—
          sweat ephemeral motes—
          bite off tongues for blood speech—
          roll upon the ground and die for them,
                make mirrors,
                fresh motes,
                maps of passage...

...and the angels, thus, feed upon decay and are the leeches of
all that we call "evil"...
...and they occur to the mind as a rising in the bake of any
thought cake—

physical fevers do levitate them surely —
thoughts of/in repetition attempt to trap them,
>   for we would feed upon angel food cake
>   (the barococo of sweet Bach's awful hunger) /
>   (gentle Gertrude Stein having her cake
>   and eating it too—

>>   the residue:
>>   "There is no
>>   repetition."...)

...*In* which—the angels move...up and down the ladders of language...with*out* moving—

out of *which*—comes the nervous endings...*this:* is it Asmodei, as H. D. would have it? :
>   "the second of the genies zodiacaux,
>   to whom one may cry,
>   *exhaussez mon incantation, ma prière...*
>   raise up, lift up, receive my recognition,
>   and this at last, with no reservation,";
>   (and is this that Asmodeus I came to know?...
>   angel of asthma?—
>   and is that why I cried reading "Hermetic Definitions"?/
>   could not, in my whole life, go beyond:
>   "what has the word done?
>   you include but in small grandeur,
>   the whole circle of the sun.")...

...*with*in which: the beg in beginnings / the thrown up pun—
all of undigestible language the angels feed upon: these *distinctions* of vision:

>>   *that / thus:*

>   the dimension of angels is a tensor—
>   the reality of angels is a surety—
>   the grasping of angels is as a disjointed leg and a blessing
for poor Jacob—
>   the handling of angels is as the hand feels itself,

in transformation,
surely moving,
to its ends...

...and the angels of fingers can be seen in the bend of light
when the tips almost touch and wherein (aura?) they seem to be
touching...

...and the angel of auras (the guardian angel?) can be seen after
staring at a yellow sheet of paper and then looking to the naked
body of another...

...and the guardian angel of self (angels of eyes?/angle of ego?
/anguish of soul?) can be the actor of seeing itself,

as I impersonates each eye
(to see the moving yellow
of all angels of the sky as
some stilled blue),
as I'll an isle become
(to bend the rays of sun's
set into renaissance perspective
for ego's grasp of the angel
of the dying of the light),
annihilation...

...and the angel at the gate of Eden is viz-ability itself...

...and its sword is the word of God—is the word of sword—is
the knowledge of shape that makes a circle of the sun...

...and the flames thereof it are that stolen light whereby the
mind's eye projects its pictures—its flickerings those rhythms of
thought itself—its fuel the decay of vision into the smoke of
memory...   and:

angels move thru the qualities of smoke in a diffraction of
the shadow of light—

the doors of darkness / home of angelical forces (as my
wife Jane has shown me, in my mind's eye, the strands of light
that stream from the shadow cast by her head)...

...and the halos of halos are the halos of angels...

[1968]

eyes

in defense of amateur

have been making films for over 15 years now. I have contributed to many commercial films as "director," "photographer," "editor," "writer," "actor" even, "grip," etcetera, and sometimes in combinations of all of these. But mostly I have worked without title, in *no* collaboration with others—I have worked alone and at home, on films of seemingly *no* commercial value...'at home' with a medium I love, making films I care for as surely as I have as a father cared for my children. As these home movies have come to be valued, have grown into a public life, I, as the maker of them, have come to be called a "professional," an "artist," and an "amateur." Of those three terms, the last one—"amateur"—is the one I am truly most honored by...even tho' it is most often used in criticism of the work I have done by those who don't understand it.

The 'professional' is always much admired in the public life of any time. He is the Don Juan whose techniques (of sex or whatever), whose conquests in terms of number, speed, duration or mathematical-whatever, whose stance for perfection (whatever can be intellectually measured to determine a competitional 'winner') does dazzle any man at any time he relates to the mass of people, does count him self as of a number, and does thus have a public life: but when that man is alone, or with those few, or that one other, he loves, his admiration of Don Juan, and of all such technicians as "professors"/"professionals" are, disappears from any consciousness he may have—except, alas, his consciousness of himself...and if he is then tempted to "lord" it with those he loves, if his "home is his castle" and he "The King" thereof it, he will soon cease to have any private life whatsoever; and he may even come to be the Don Juan himself, forever in "the hell" of the admiration of other people's public life. He will, as such, tend to always think of himself as "on display": and if he makes movies, even if only in his home, he will be known for making a great "show" of it and will imitate the trappings of the commercial cinema (usually with no success whatsoever, as he will attempt the grandiose of visual *and* audio with penny-whistle means); and he will buy equipment beyond any need or real joy in it (usually penny-dreadful- junk-stage-props for the 'production' of his imaginary profession...rather than for any loving *re*-production of the movements of his living): and his wife and/or impatient friends will be expected take his egocentric directions, to labor under his delusions, to come to "grips" *for* him (as laziness is usually a sign of professional egocentricity which would have some servant to follow its every aspiration with a director's chair to sit in); and his children or whomever will be expected to "grin and bear" his every pompous set-up and staged dramatics (to the expense, as usual, of any real play)...ah, well—we all do really know him, this would-be professional, who does in his imitation of "productions" give us a very real symbol of the limitations of commercial cinema without any of the accomplishments thereof that endeavor: the best we can hope for such a man is that either he goes on into commercial filmmaking and takes all such professionalism out of his home (where he might become amateur again) or else that he makes an obvious fool of himself (whereupon he becomes lovable again to those who love him).

Now, as to the term: "artist": I've come to the conclusion, after years of struggling to determine the meaning of this word, that anyone becomes an artist the instant he *feels* he is—perhaps even the instant he *thinks* he is—and that, therefore, almost everyone, some time or other in his living, is an artist. A public Artist, with capitol "A," is as much admired by many, and of as little value to an individual life, as any professional. It is a word, in our current usage, very like the word "love." When

Love is capped, it applies to Mother, Father, Sister, Brother, Wife, Children, Lover and—as also capped and usually prefaced by a "possessive" word—"your" country, "my" dog (even "yours," "love me, love my dog," etc.), "his" favorite food, "our" friendship, club, etc.—and, thus, the word comes to have very little public meaning...just as the word "Art" applied to craftsmanship, cleverness, or facility of any competitive kind ceases to have any special meaning what-so-ever: but both words continue to move with the deepest meaning that individual intonation can give them in the privacy of every single living utterance of each of them with personal meaning...that is the beauty of both these words—and that is why I do no more care to be called an artist, except by my friends and those who love me, than I would care to be called a lover, publicly.

"Amateur" is a word which, in the Latin, meant "lover": but today it has become a term like "Yankee" ("Amateur—Go Home"), hatched in criticism, by professionals who so little understand the value of the word or its meaning that they do honor it, and those of us who identify with it, *most* where they think to shame and disgrace in their usage of it.

An amateur works according to his own necessity (a Yankee-enough proclivity) and is, in that sense, "at home" anywhere he works: and if he takes pictures, he photographs what he loves or needs in some-such sense—surely a more real, and thus honorable, activity than work which is performed for some gain or other than what the work itself gives...surely more personally meaningful than work only accomplished for money, or fame, power, etc....and *most* assuredly more individually meaningful than commercial employment—for the true amateur, even when in consort with other amateurs, is always working alone, gauging his success according to his care for the work rather than according to the accomplishments or recognitions of others.

Why then have critics, teachers, and other guardians of the public life come to use the term derogatorily? Why have they come to make "amateur" mean : "inexperienced," "clumsy," "dull," or even "dangerous"? It is because an amateur is one who really lives his life—not one who simply "performs his duty"—and as such he experiences his work while he's work-ing—rather than going to school to learn his work so he can spend the rest of his life just doing it dutifully—; and the ama-teur, thus, is forever learning and growing thru his work into all his living in a "clumsiness" of continual discovery that is as beautiful to see, if you have lived it and *can* see it, as to watch young lovers in the "clumsiness" of their lack of knowing and the joy of their continual discovery of each other, if you have ever loved and can appreciate young lovers without jealousy. Amateurs and lovers are those who look on beauty and liken themselves to it, thus say they "like it": but professionals, and especially critics, are those who feel called-upon and duty-bound to profess, prove, improve, etc., and are therefore es-tranged from any simplicity of reception, acception, or open-ness at all unless they are over-whelmed by something. *Beauty* overwhelms only in the form of *drama;* and *love* over-whelms only when it has become *possessive.* It is The Critic in each man that does give credence to The Professional Critic's stance against The Amateur, for when any man feels ashamed of the lack of drama in his "home-movies," he does put some-thing of his shame into his making (or his talking about the pictures he's taken) and does, thus, achieve the drama of embar-rassment. And when an amateur filmmaker does feel vulner-able because of the open-ness of the love-expression he has made in photographing his wife and children he tends to shame himself for the simplicity of his vision of beauty and to begin to hide that simple sight thru a complexity of photographic tricks and staged cutenesses, to give his "home movies" a veneer, a slick and impenetrable "hide" and/or to devise filmic jokes at the expense of himself and his loved ones—as if to protect himself and his images from criticism by making them *obviously*

foolish…as if to say: "Look, I *know* I'm a fool—I *intend* to make
you laugh at me and my pictures!" Actually, this latter proclivity
at its ultimate is one of the most endearing qualities of ama-
teurism, but also, like any self- protectiveness, it prevents a
deeper experiencing and knowledge of the person and his films
and, indeed, of the whole amateur filmmaking medium. It
makes "home movies" endearing like fat, jolly people who obscure their features in flesh and their feelings in jokes and laughter at their expense—thus protecting themselves from the
in-depth involvement with others: and, then too, the amateur
film does often beg for attention in ways that impose upon any
viewer, force him to a hypocritical "kindness," and preclude any
real attention…like the stutterer who can hold a roomful of
people to a constrained silence as he struggles to come to
speech. Yet the stutterer is very often worth waiting for and attending carefully precisely because his speech-difficulty can
tend to make him think twice before struggling with utterance
and can condition him to speak only when he has something
absolutely necessary to say…he will obviously never 'profess'
and is, thus, automatically a lover of spoken language.

I suggest the conscious cultivation of an *honest* pride in all
"neurotics" (rather than any therapy which would imply the
ideal of some "normalcy" or other) *and* in the "neurotic" medium of "home-movie" making (rather than any professorial
tutoring which might set a goal of some norm of filmmaking).
I would like to see "fat" films carry their own weight of meaning and stuttery montages reflect the meaningfullness of repetition, the acts of mis-take as integral steps in motion picture
taking. Mistakes in filming, like Freudian "slips" in language,
"puns" and the like, very often contain the meaning that was
covered-up thru error as well as the reason for erring. When
mother-in-law is "accidently" superimposed over images of the
family dog, a pride in one's own wit (rather than self-conscious
embarrassment) can free both filmmaker and his medium thru

recognition of delightful confession and inform him and his mother-in-law of a relationship that could, as always, change for the better if both are capable of facing the truth...besides, when such a *super*-imposition as that is treated as a meaningless joke or embarrassing mistake, the derogatory suggestion is the *only* one noticed ("Well...is *that* what you think of me—ha! ha! ha!," mother-in-law will say) and never the positive aspects (such as the amateur's affection for his dog, for instance). As we are all much conditioned by language, many technical errors refer to the name of the technique via visual/language "puns" (as, for instance, a man may take a picture of his wife "over-exposed" when she was wearing a dress with a neck-line he considered too low) and even pictures that depend primarily upon referential words for their full meaning (as, I'm convinced, most amateurs tend to photograph a tree on the far left of the film frame with an even arrangement of rocks and bushes extending horizontally from left to right to approximate the look of the word "Tree"). I find these references to language constrictive filmmaking (as most movie pans are left-to-right because of the habit pattern of reading) as finally rather obscure from a visual standpoint: but one must be aware of them in order to break the habit of them: and awareness actually begins in some taking pride in the accomplishments of these linguistic visions. And some filmmakers will enjoy these word-oriented pictures (that *I* find "constricting") and make them consciously: but either way, shame will never end a habit or make it a conscious virtue; but it will, rather, obscure the process and pot-bind its roots beyond any possibilities of growth.

The artificial "tricks" with which amateurs tend to hide their real feelings do, like "mis-takes," tend to contain-thru-method the very truth they were effected to conceal; and they are, in fact, consciously contrived puns or metaphors. I, personally, do very much care for the whole area of technical innovation in filmmaking: and I am very often accused of being too "tricky" in my motion picture making. It is certainly a proclivity I am conscious of: and I only run the personal risk of taking *too great* a pride in technical trickery. To counteract this danger to my own growth, I make it a point *never to contrive* a "trick," an effect, or a technical virtuosity, but only permit myself *to arrive* at a filmic innovation when it arises from the felt needs of the film itself in the making and as an absolute necessity of realizing my emotions in the act of motion picture making. I try very hard to be honest with myself about this; and I can usually discipline myself most clearly by making all technical explorations the direct expression of acts of seeing (rather than making an image to-be-seen). For instance, when I photographed the births of my children I saw that with their first in-takes of breath their whole bodies were suffused with rainbowing colors from head to toe: but the film stock always recorded only the spread of reddish blotches across the surface of the skin: and so, by the time I had photographed the birth of my third child and in each occasion seen this incredible phenomenon, I felt compelled to paint some approximation of it directly on the surface of the 16mm film and superimposed, as it were, over the photographed images of birth. As I had no way to prove whether this vision of skin rainbows at birth was a hallucination of mine or an extent reality too subtle for photographic recording, I felt free while editing this third birth film to also paint, on each 16mm frame at a time, all the visions of my mind's eye and to inter-cut with the birth pictures some images I had remembered while watching the birth—some pictures of a Greek temple, polar bears, and flamingos (from a previous film of mine)...images which had, of course, no real existence at the time of the birth except in my "imagination" (a word from the Greek meaning: "image birth") but were, all the same, *seen* by *me* as surely as was the birth of the baby (were, in fact, given-birth-to- by me in an interior act of mimetic magic as old as the recorded history of Man.)

All of which brings us to the question of symbolism and

subject matter in "home-movie" making. When an amateur photographs scenes of a trip he's taking, a party or other special occasion, and especially when he's photographing his children, he's primarily seeking a *hold on time* and, as such, is ultimately attempting to defeat death. The entire act of motion picture making, thus, can be considered as an *exteriorization* of the process of *memory.* "Hollywood," sometimes known as "the dream factory," makes ritualistic-dramas in celebration of mass memory—very like the rituals of tribal people—and wishful-thinking movies which seek to control the national destiny...as sure as primitive tribes throw water on the ground to bring rain...and they make "social" or "serious" dramas, at great commercial risk to the industry, as a corporate act of "sacrifice" —not unlike the practices of self-torture priests undergo in order to "appease the gods": and the whole commercial industry has created a pseudo church whose "god" is "mass psychology" and whose anthropomorphism consists of praying *to* ("Buy this—**NOW!**"), and preying *upon* (polling, etc.) "the-greatest-number-of-people" as if, thereby, the human destiny were predictable and/or could be controlled thru mimicry. But the amateur photographs the persons, places, and objects of his love and the events of his happiness and personal importance in a gesture that *can* act directly and solely according to the needs of memory. He does not have to invent a god *of* memory, as does the professional: nor does the amateur have to appease any personification of God in his making. He is free, if he but accept the responsibility of his freedom, to work as the spirit of his god, or his memory, or his particular needs, move him. It is for this reason that I believe any art of the cinema must inevitably arise from the amateur, "home-movie" making medium. And I believe that the so-called "commercial," or ritual, cinema must inevitably take its cues from the films of amateurs rather than, as is too often the case these days, the other way round.

I now work equally in 8 and 16 millimeter making mostly

silent films (and am even making a 35mm film at home); I am guided primarily in all creative dimensions by the spirit of the home in which I'm living, by my own very living room. I have bought some 8 and 16mm films which sit alongside books and LP records on my library shelf and I have sold many of my 8mm films to both private homes and public libraries—thus by-passing the theatrical limitations of film viewing entirely...thus creating a circumstance wherein films may be lived-with and studied in depth—returned-to again and again like poetry and recorded music.

I am currently working on a long "home-movie" war film in 8mm: I discovered that the television set was as crucial a part of my living- therefore working-room as the walls of it and its various other furnishings, and that T.V. could present me with as necessary an involvement as the activities of my children: ergo, I finally had to deal with its primary impulse at present—The War—as surely, as an amateur, as I would with any and every important occasion of our living. I carry a camera (usually 8mm) with me on almost every trip away from the house (even to the grocery store) and thus become camera-laden 'tourist' of my own immediate environment as well as in those distant places I travel to—(many 8mm cameras fit easily into a coat pocket or purse and are, thus, no more of a burden than a transistorized radio)...and I call these home and travel movies "SONGS," as they are to me the recorded visual music of my inner and exterior life—the "fixed" melodies of, the filmic memory of, my living.

[1971]

manifest

Let me warn once more and then be silent, dark time coming.

(The so-called "dark ages" simply thus/that folk forgot how to dye and thereby came clothed dulled shades gray shags of animal black etcetera, even kings lacking purple—longlivethe king! — till the secret thought was won again and juice of rock wrung and again the fabric of daily life was as flowers.)

Let me then warn that those who would/could restrict our perimeters have drawn lines; and they are these:

that all which is personally perceptible be suspect

(as is immeasurable Color accorded "secondary citizenship" within the hierarchy Science)

that that which is person-privately shareable, tralal, be circumscribed -sized -shaped and weighted by/as commune *all*, Tradit!

(as it is with Sex past tense now taught future participle)

that The Personae, that greek form whereby innerdividual might surface in The Pub. true semblence-of-self, be thought as false as "mask" meaning "screen" to hide or lie behind.

(as The Truth comes to be made to mean the agreed-upon-fact) that a person, I, be finally unthinkable

(as Art is).

I take it that The Arts afford the last ungoverned public surfacing of Person and constitute thus the greatest threat to those who feel they could/ should enslave sensibility,

just as I know Sex to be that first/last move person-to-person beyond governmentality—

truths always, yet!, personally *colored* beyond measurability...

those who rule hate these truths;

this my warning:

:   that we not be lulled, as was Garcia Lorca whose last words to his cell-mate were, "Don't worry–they don't shoot poets."

: that we not be fooled by governmental Sup. for Artists (it's U.S.ence simply this/that:

(1) having made patronage tax deductible, all act of Personal Gen. was subvert to greed.

: (2) having made tax deduct. more and more than difficult Xcept as inst. to inst. shuffles money—see so-called Tax Reform Bill '69—Person was jettisoned in the transact altogether...artists effectively herded into UNIverse Cities or "left"(UNsupported)out,

: (3) it managed that ONLY bureaucratic Wash. could pick up the rest/"right" cards upon the tabled Arts
so that

: (4) these sacred first/last acts of inner-dependence would be played as if 'twere hobby or per-choice escapist occupation—useful to keep the increasingly leisured discontents from making bombs...(the funds most natch going thus to education, workshops, art fairs, sports-sort competitions and the like).

Anybody for free-verse circumspect finger-only painting homey-movie build-it-yrself archycraft sing-along play act?

Artists!, like they say: let's have *at* it!—all pretense (pre the tendency) we can teach 'em how-to-do-it half-aesthetically... The Muses be made Amuse(govern)ment! "It's a living," say the walking dead. "If you can't beat 'em?"...Fuck 'em.

Most hopeful sign: the *real* young (trapped as I too much am in these schools for *act*ual Youth) those few of them who *really* call my attention (most usually first by the shyness of 'em) do very deliberately shunt publight and all complicity as could be tabbed "a movement" (thus demeaned); and after a good look to and at me, and my contemporaries in The Arts, they sympathetically declare they'll keep it/art absolutely private and/or share theirs only as one would love among one's friends.

Thus I'm coming to believe that as it is in the hopechests and closets of Russ. & China so it will be here for similarity's sake—world's social norm this 20th Cent.   *[1974]*

Thigh Line Lyre Triangular

the seen

I have believed for many years and come to believe more and more the older I get that the art is given as a gift through persons' urgency. And that the responsibility of the artist is to be personal enough. That this gift, this that he or she could not arrive at along a train of logical thought can just come to exist along a line of...shaping itself according to the extent of the maker's experience and no more. That is, that it not pitch over into ego or that a maker begins to shape him or herself according to cleverness or whatever. Certainly there is no work that more confirms me in that sense than *The Text of Light*. For me it is most clearly of all things a gift given to me to make. I really have found only two things to say about it that illuminate what I was involved in; one is almost as a prayer bead or a constant reassurance I returned to Johannes Scotus Erigena's "All that is is light." Secondly, William Blake's "To find a world in a grain of sand." These two things were very helpful in actually a very practical sense to help me hold to the promises of this film and fulfill them at least to the best of the ability that I have. So beyond that I really haven't anything, any clarities, and will look forward to some of your questions expanding my thought about this work. I don't in any sense think of it as my own and to an extraordinary sense I never was able to kid myself that it was my own.

How did you make it?

I was trying very hard to make a portrait. I am getting involved in portraits. I have known a man since high school and he subsequently became a multimillionaire. So for years we were separated in that way that millionaires and artists are separated. Finally we overcame that separation, and as this is an art school I think this is a valuable piece of information how we did it. I

declared to him that I would never under any circumstances accept any money from him; and in such a firm and full way that
he knew I meant it. Then we could be friends. To a man with a
great deal of money, a poor man is a bottomless pit. So from
that point on it became very interesting, the relationship, because his world was totally distinct from mine and was quite a
mystery. In fact the American businessman is a real bogeyman.
So along the line of doing the Pittsburgh trilogy on police, hospitals, and at the morgue, I was determined to get a portrait of
an American businessman if possible, and that it would be a
rare opportunity, and that here was someone I had known since
high school and there was a chance. So I was trying to photograph him in his office and he, terribly embarrassed, was blow-
ing great clouds of Cuban cigar smoke and obscuring
everything and I was failing. And it was interesting because I
had a macro lens on, which I was using as a kind of distance
lens. It has a bellows. And I was failing and the camera slumped
forward and the lens bent sort of with the bellows and it seemed
hopeless. But I have the habit to always look into the lens before
moving the camera. So I looked and saw what seemed to me at
first a forest. And I thought, my god, where is this coming from?
And looked more close. And I called my friend around and he
looked and was astonished and then I looked again and it had
changed and a stream was running through it. Then I saw that
the lens was pointed at his ash tray. So I began taking single
frames of his ash tray. And he is so lovely a man he accommo-
dated this. In fact he's so witty a man that he invited people to go
on with conference meetings on business & what not & I went
right on photographing this ash tray. His office also is such a
location & construction that it has sun all day long. He has windows all round, from dawn to sunset there is wonderful sun
pouring into this office. So I just began moving from window to
window of this office, and Helen, his secretary, got very excited
and brought other pieces of glass; which at first, only not to

hurt her feelings, I set kind of around the ash tray. Then I noticed that if I touched the very outer-most piece of glass out
here, it very often changed what was in the ash tray. Then someone brought in the grand...so proudly, brought in a crystal ball.
And this I put in the center of the ash tray. And there was finally
a collection of very fine crystal all around the ash tray, and
sometimes a little bit in the ash tray, and this way and that way
and the crystal ball, and all this was in the sun of course, just
shined beautifully and I went on clicking away, most of the film
a frame at a time throughout that summer.

Once I remember somebody came to a business conference
and they walked through the room and he said to Gordon, kind
of very, "What's he doing?" And Gordon without a break in
stride just said, "He's photographing our ash trays." This began
to help him in business because people became so confused and
disturbed at what was this mystery that he had the business edge
on them. So it worked out fine for everybody. Except I made one
error which I must point out. I became so obsessed with this ash
tray that I bent over all summer and ruptured one, possibly two
disks. So that's why I have this cane. And anyway it was worth it.

I saw you one of the last times you were here and you were showing
The Act of Seeing with One's Own Eyes. *And before showing it
you said it was nothing to be afraid of, it was only about light hitting
objects and bouncing back and seeing it with your eyes. And I was interested in why after using light in such a very exquisite, definitive way you
wanted to use it in a way that was so unarticulated, that was so abstract.*

Well, she is telling me in the form of a question that she
thinks my film is unarticulated with respect to light. And I must
disagree, that this film is called *The Text of Light* because in that
ash tray I found a way to create an equivalent of many behaviors
of light that I have observed, that are not recognized by science,
and in fact I suppose would be considered mad by some of the
less generous scientists of our time. But I will name a few that

therefore, that because they are not recognized by science we are not trained to observe; and not very many people have seen these, though some have.

I have seen that before a rainstorm there are light-like streaks that come down through the air that are metaphors of rain though they are not wet. In fact have held my hand and some of them come through that hand with no sense of moisture and of course the fact that the streak goes right through the hand is itself clear that it's not raining. And then rain will follow. And because I live in a place where many clouds pass over and most do not rain, I had a way to check myself. Could I tell within 30 seconds to a minute if it was going to rain or not and invariably I could because always, if that cloud was going to rain, it was preceded by these light-like...they would be streaks as if you would see a tiny streak of light or spark in a dark room only they would be bluish Though they could be yellowish also. Those are interchangeable colors anyway, optically. They could be yellowish.

Then I have seen light-like phosphorescence move horizontally along the ground, as a wind. And I have seen it pool, as if a pool of phosphorescent image. Then I have seen sometimes that streaks shoot up from these pools or from the very ground. Again light-like and ephemeral like a phosphorescence in daylight which makes shapes, shapes of plants. And I have seen this quite a bit in the spring on just dirt and I have seen a similarity of plant grow up in this place. I have seen—as Kirlian photography almost touches on now, and maybe does—I have seen leaves spark or emit a spark-like emanation at their edges that are offshoots directly of the veins within that leaf, and therefore as that leaf then grows, do create a metaphor previous to the actual extension of these veins. These things I have seen, one, because I have been involved with seeing all my life and I'm really open to seeing all there is when I'm well. Two, because somewhere along the line I realized something that was constricting my sight in this pursuit: which was my training in this society in renaissance perspective—in that form of seeing we could call "westward-hoing man's," which is to try to clutch a landscape or the heavens or whatever. That is a form of sight which is aggressive & which seeks to make of any landscape a piece of real estate. In fact the irony that we have so named property our Real Estate demonstrates the western limitation. I would like to see science make a check of the eyes, of the musculature of eastern peoples, let's say as distinct from ours. I believe it would be quite distinct. This search for this form of grasping sight has created a powerful musculature to permit that. And too as is necessary to permit us to drive on these thruways and to move with this mobility among these constructions supportive of that renaissance perspective.

Well, that pursuit is wonderful in itself, and it is of course my native pursuit, but on the other hand it has the problem that it is exclusive of all other kinds of seeing. So what I'm trying to get at, in order to see these things I have to be in an extraordinary relaxed state of seeing. Then all other kinds of seeing become immediately possible and of great involvement with the light of course. And I believe, not only do I believe with Johannes Scotus Erigena that "All that is is light," but I even think that a wonderful thing has happened in our time and passed almost unnoticed. That a dialog beginning with him and reaching a public prominence in the thirteenth century in the writings of Grosseteste... Dig that name. The first man whom they tried to put down with the name Bighead. So he picked it right up and made them understand that it was so. And then later Duns Scotus and then of course Francis Bacon who is better known ...who came and tidied up a whole lot of things and therefore is better known. But this brilliance of these Light Philosophies, English philosophers, who because of their feelings stated in words that: *thought was illumination.* I mean the last run down of what they did is in the comic strips when somebody's supposed to have an idea: they make a lightbulb. But they felt their thinking was electrical or light-like. Now hundreds of years have passed and finally an enormous construct of science which would seem to be antagonistic to such thinking has permitted Niels Bohr and Riemann and of course Albert Einstein to prove, within that structure, that matter is still light. Light held in a bind. So what this ash tray permitted me to do was to photograph equivalence of things seen and processes of evolution, of ephemerality of light taking shape and finally taking a very solid seeming shape. Along a line of exactitude. When the film is seen on this level, it's even pedantic.

I was wondering if you actually saw the spectrum through the view-finder, through the lens?

Yes, I saw very much what you saw on the screen, only it was better of course. Because in the meantime it has passed through ...only what Eastman Kodak film would accept has been taken down, only what the lab didn't botch has been left on the strip. Then it similarly has had to pass through an interneg, and finally come to a print. So if you enjoyed this, then go look in an ash tray, or something. Because it's much better. How it's been able to pass through me so that it can be called a "text" is that I have been true to my appreciation & understanding of light operating in every day life in these fashions, i.e. preceding matter. I even believe it precedes animal motion. I have not seen that enough to be sure of it. But I believe that there is a form or at least certain kinds of gestures are preceded by a flash of light-like emanation. I mean this is very exciting to me, in fact it's...you see I've been reading Johannes Scotus Erigena and his later "echo," Duns Scotus, since Ezra Pound gave them to me at 18 or something. But it seems we are so trained in this society to read something and keep that quite separate from the living experience. So I thought it was wonderful but I didn't believe it. And then finally I came to see. And now I have had, through this ash tray, the opportunity to present an equivalent of it. And if you think about it, this is the most normal film in the world. Because here I am with a macro lens, which is a piece of glass here, and one stuck way out here, or several. And they are never more than an inch or two away from a crystal ash tray which is surrounded by other glass, so where does the lens end? That *all* could be considered a lens which is photographing the sun; and that's all that makes these shapes on the screen. And that's very exciting.

My question has to do with what you said earlier. You said it had to do with a relaxed way of seeing and I was trying to get back to what you are now saying about seeing the ash tray. In my mind it seems the relaxed way of seeing comes about through the high excitement way of seeing.

Well I would agree with you because I don't, by "relaxed," mean flaccid. And I avoid the word "meditation" because it has certain eastern connotations which in this society are usually misunderstood. So we need another word. What I'm doing in photographing this ash tray for instance, I'm sitting for hours to get 30 seconds of film. I'm sitting watching what's happening and clicking a frame, and sitting and watching, and further than that, I had shot several hundred feet and they seemed dead. They didn't reflect at all my excitement and emotion and feeling. They had no anima in them. Except for two or three shots where the lens which was on a tripod, pressed against the desk, had jerked. Those were just random, but that gave me the clue. What I began doing was always holding the camera in hand. For hours. Clicking. Waiting. Seeing what the sun did to the scene. As I saw what was happening in the frame to these little particles of light, changing, I would shift the camera very slightly. If you want to know how slightly you have to realize I was never photographing in an area bigger than this 4th fingernail. You couldn't tap the camera. It had to be moved by a quivering atten-

tion of the hand. That took maybe 13 or 14 moves over a period
of ten minutes. Then to get that in mind: what *it* was doing and
changing and how I was dancing with it had to be extended in
memory; one, how that would come out at 24 frames a second
and two, as to, was the dance real?

And all the time I was doing this I had to have a friendly
argument in my mind with Jordan Belson who I knew would
hate just exactly this. He would say, Oh wonderful what it is, but
why is it jerky? Or why not centered? Or, you know...and to
hold myself together I would say, No, Jordon, it has to be this
way. So I, I owe him very much. He sustained me in that way a
beautiful argument can, because it was very much in his territory. I mean this film is very much on his side of the street.

Though there is another man. I want to mention that the
film is dedicated to Jim Davis. I suddenly one night had this
overwhelming feeling... I got mad because someone had written an article on many people working with the so-called abstract film, which term I don't believe in anyway. But they had
not mentioned Jim Davis, and he has always resisted being mentioned. It is true, he's a very shy man. He had lived all his life, the
last 20 years at 44 Wiggins Street, in Princeton, N.J., very ill with
diabetes and with a lot of back trouble and in bed the last decade. With his great construct before him, so that from his bed
he could photograph whenever his constructs created a light
pattern that seemed real to him, refracted light. He was literally
the first man who had shown me refracted light on film. So I
called him up and asked him if I could dedicate the film to him.
And I was surprised that he didn't say no; but I'm so glad I did
because he was dead a week later. Almost totally ignored. So he
is someone to be looked at now that he's dead.

*I just want to follow that up...I think that most people are part-time
filmmakers. And it's the moment of high excitement in which you realize you've got something there. As I watched this film for example, I*

have very severe night blindness, as I watched this film I began to real-ize how important this night blindness is to me.

Oh yes, wonderful.

I was able to see a lot of things I never associated with that. It's the high excitement of the moment of capturing something which is so critically important to pass on to people. It's not to analyse in a philosophical way.

Yes, I appreciate that: only it depends on how you use information. I mean, most people misuse philosophy worse than any other discipline in this time. And yet, I am very defi-cient in reading philosophy.

Part of that, I was pre-prejudiced that this was the dullest area on earth by a series of very dull teachers. And only a very dear friend, Forrest Williams, who happens to be here tonight, has maybe saved me; and I would like to pass on to you, in phi-losophy you can find the most practical information in the world. You see, this line, "All that is is light" as translated by Pound & threads its way through the *Cantos*—many thoughts have moved along this line as if it's a very solid string. So it led me to the possibilities of this film. Now you say other people in the room want to make films and what will lead them? I don't know because that is truly a personal matter. And that's what excites me. Because it took me all these years to realize I could never be anything but personal. So then I had to ask myself, What did I think I was being those other times? Well…I thought I was being a good boy, and behaving myself, as I had been trained to do, and was continually encouraged for it, in fact threatened by every institute I've passed through. Be it school or job or whatever. And of course constantly by the overwhelming power of the government that is…I mean…the only contender left in the newspapers for equal space with the government, however stupid it becomes, is the sports field. And both of them move inexorably like a Chinese water torture against any con-cept of person. Sports move against it by putting the whole em-phasis on teamwork to destroy the concept of play. That is the most vicious of all. Because little kids get that first. Play is extensive & absolutely individual until it becomes part of a game and then the game is created to pitch two masses of people against each other in competition. Then the government—I mean I don't need to speak about the government in this year, my god, but...

Someone asked me recently, Why have you struggled so hard to see and ended up so different from your neighbors...or something...who do you think you are? I said quite truly, To save my life! I knew they were trying to kill me and so when I first knew this I developed asthma at one year old. Which gave my mother a lot of other things to do. She was trying to use me because she had adopted me to save the marriage; and I'd failed. So she had for her efforts a child constantly wheezing. Then I moved to protect my skin surface—I was very fat, so I was again buffered against all this use as much as possible. Then I developed sinus trouble which shut off the nose. Ear aches, glasses. Get the picture? By the time I was six...I escaped sports because I developed a hernia. The problem was that life wasn't worth living with all these tactics. So the next thing to do was get it all together and stop all this disease. In this society I think, for many, illness has been the only way to get through. And it may be one reason I have this back problem at this moment. Because the pressure is very heavy on me at this time. This may be. And if so, that's great because then I'll come to terms with it and find some other way and get rid of that too.

It has been—what I'm trying to say is that is has been a desperate struggle to keep alive. And to keep alive to me meant that I had to be personal, which is all that I could be. But then, having said all that, I want to say also, persons also wish to be social. So then the social inclinations come out. Like, I can understand that persons want to drive on the right side of the road or the left side so they don't run into each other. And I understand also of course, finally came with great difficulty to beginning to under-

stand the miracle of loving, another. And that was very hard
with this route that I took. That may have a lot to do with why I
am an artist. And by "artist" I mean someone who makes
things under/in trance. Things which can be looked at over and
over again, or experienced again & again. Will last. Otherwise
you can throw out the term "art" and I don't care. And I think I
came to be able to make that because I had, was so locked in,
that I was exploding with things. With feelings and thoughts
that I wanted to get out. Then the way to get them out was the
same as, I mean...Morton Subotnick visited recently and told
me that he thought the birth of music was the scream. Two
things: the scream goes to the greatest pitch that it can, but one
cannot sustain that scream. So then the tone would drop way
down low to provide a bass which can be held forever. Then a
scale is established in between. My sense of it was that it began
with the heartbeat which was overwhelming. That some man,
woman, creature had to beat upon the chest to get it out, and
stamp on the ground and then found a hollow log and then
stretched skin over it. And you could send it for miles. Let's
make love or war or whatever. So it's always that real—the need
to get something internal exteriorized; and whatever the exterior is can only be an equivalent. No drum in the world, not even
a stethoscope, will actually make the sound of the heart that
you hear yourself in your own ears...and when it's pounding
...it's pounding and it may fly out of your chest and everyone
else is going around and they don't *hear* it—you see. But if someone screams, people pay attention. And if they give it a form,
they'll pay attention again and again. Then the miracle is, it's
wonderful, this which otherwise just would be an egocentric
trick...then people start listening to their own screams and
heartbeats. Then to me, that's the point.

I fear people getting hung up over art. That is, getting excited
about art and just looking at art. To me, always an expression
made out of such desperation and taking such a form, and leap-

ing beyond what that person himself could arrive at; that is being informed by what you can call the muses, or god, or the angels or the subconscious, whatever you like. But something in
the work process comes through, that I am not capable of
thinking along the line of thought. It seems as if it comes from
elsewhere; it does not seem as if it comes from me. But it only
comes, strangely and ironically, when I am being the most personal that I can be. Where I tell a story that's more unique to me,
a unique story like something happening to me that nobody ever
heard of happening to anybody else. Then I know more that I
am a person. And that's a very strong string for the unconscious,
the angels or muses to play upon.

It's caused me an awful lot of trouble, and made me very
lonely that I see light behaving in ways that not very many other
people see. And the ash tray, and this force that moves through
such an experience gave me a way to exteriorize that. So I am
very grateful.

*What about these flashes of light; do you ever see gestures, flashes of
light, is that in the film itself?*
No, it's not photographable.
Is this in mind?
No, but that is an interesting question. What part of these
visions are feedback fantasy, which is always just a mix, or an
Irish stew of memories actually? So the mind can project out of
the memory pot all kinds of mixes that do not directly reflect a
creature you'll see on earth, but...
*What I'm talking about, is if you were in this last state you are talking
about, would you be able to see what kind of mood I was in?*
Well, if I were relaxed and in my home, and able to relax to
that extent and see, maybe. I do see auras, is that what you mean?
All the time?
Well, no. I have to drive on the freeways and make a living
and so on. And I'm subject also to these ordinary pressures...

the world as it is. Which socially is, in my opinion, awful. I really feel that the human animal is up against the most intensive drive ever, to stamp out any sensibility of animal life. And, ah, people being persons. And I do feel it's so serious that I think the last public surfacing of persons is through the arts. And of course now, having been unable to starve out the artists, now the government is moving to create, ah, institutes to quote help the arts end quote, and which will, to some extent, do that; but I am very fearful of what the intent is in the long run. In fact I'm not fearful at all, I know exactly what the intent is in the long run of this process. So the hope is they will be stupid—like all other forms of government—and will fail. But the intent is really...there is a greater fear, among those who rule, of the arts, than there is of any political opposition. Because the opposition can be, even in a revolution, can be honored. They will behave in all respects like those in power. If they get in power and succeed, they will certainly behave like those in power. And history has shown this again and again, & how anyone can have any hope in a revolution after reading any history at all, I don't know. Hope springs eternal, but, I mean, really... On the other hand, the extent to which people within a culture primarily recognize themselves as persons, is *not* controllable. That cannot be massed, except under real emergency. That is, except when there really is an attack on that culture which requires everyone to be massed.

Unfortunately, it is not that there are twelve dirty old men in Washington trying to destroy us all; it is that there is in most people, through a cultural inheritance, an automatic wish to be governed and to govern others. And the government...and so that's the problem. That this is a long-going thing that people tend to seem to feel that they need. The government is just the most...they're the last ones to know anything about anything anyway. But they are the symbol. They are the anchor down of this proclivity. And the arts, artists in this century seem to make the only stance against this. They do this not because they are wiser or braver or anything, but simply because no one has ever figured out how to make a *thing that will last* without being desperately personal during the making & throughout. So you just couldn't...it's inconceivable to me that it could be done any other way—though governments will try to have things done that they will try to sell as art...which are done in exactly the opposite way. So that's the struggle. And you could either regard it as very sad that you live in this time or as very interesting. I do one or the other depending on whether I think I'm going to make it or not...

About personal desperation...you were saying you have to get it out. In your earliest stuff it seems like that was reflective of your repression, the things that were suppressed in you...why you had those different illnesses or whatever. Now I was wondering...it doesn't seem like you're trying to say personally through yourself, maybe...or mass repressiveness...

No, I'm not. I don't understand mass actually, finally. I think that is just a meaningless word...though I'm confronted by it, meaningless or not. Most of the words we read in the newspapers are meaningless in that context and we are confronted by them, and they can actually cause things which will kill you. So whether they have any meaning anymore or not, or especially that they don't, one still has to deal with them.

No, what I mean is, you said, right, you thought your parents were going to kill you—or now you're concerned that the government or the mass will kill you.

No, I'm not concerned with the government killing me. I'm concerned with me killing myself. Because of this proclivity to govern. And therefore being tricked out, or responsive to, anyone else's desire to govern, of which the primary symbol might be a Texas cop some dark night. Or some name in the newspapers. I mean I don't sit and worry about...I don't have nightmares of Gerald Ford trying to kill me.

Really, I mean it's wonderful to live. And what worries me
the most is that so much of the time I don't want to live, and so
then I try to figure out why. Why not? Or for instance one of the
prominent forms is that I go to the movies about twice a week.
Now why? That's just an escape. And what could be more ridiculous when life is so short anyway to spend a lot of time
around money and effort escaping. Then of course I get clues,
like when I'm on a lecture tour and have to go to the faculty
cocktail and it goes on and on and on. Then I stumble back to
my motel in Poughkeepsie late at night and I'm desperate for
the Tonite Show.

Then I know why I go to the escape movies also. Or why...
see I set out on almost every trip with about three books. One is
usually a poetry book; the second will be history or maybe some
book in that area, an instructive book; and the third, a detective
novel. Two days into the trip I...I mean, after I've got through
being X-rayed and all the cattle herding of the airplane port,
I'm already through with the poetry and I'm into the history.
And by the time I've had a day on the road, I'm down to the
detective novel. But I don't accept that.

Is there any personal reason why you're not signing your films now?
You see when I first signed films it was because I was making
the personal statement really, that is, my signature. That was so
long ago, you have to understand, and to scratch a signature on
film had some very powerful meaning at that time that really
distinguished it from the Hollywood film or any other kind of
film. So I've done that for years, but now as of the last couple of
years, and certainly this year, I had arrived at a place where I felt
that that had become ego-centric. For one thing my name unfortunately is not as much, is not...I don't...I'm not enabled to have
as personal a sense of my name as I did, because I've seen it too
often in print. And people have used it as a symbol in a way that
has nothing to do with person too much. And that's robbed me

of that signature to some extent. Two, which is perhaps more important, should be in the first place, I came to sense that, as of the last several years, I've become more & more convinced that I don't make them. So it began to seem ego-centric to sign them. I felt I had the right to copyright them. It's interesting that this came up at the same point that I decided to copyright. I won't do that for very many years, but I wanted to leave something to the children. And that's the only way I could do it. Everything else is in public domain. And I don't want to leave them a fortune, but a little edge. So for a few years I will copyright films. Now the interesting thing is it doesn't bother me at all, which surprised me, that it says copyright 1974 by Stan Brakhage. Oddly I seem to have that right now because I'm not so stupid as to think I have the right to sign them.

Now that's all quite special, but there's a lot of thought and tortured feeling and feeling all the line of it for me. That's how I've arrived at that. I've bracketed the film in copyright, which I don't actually have to do, but I did it because I really want to put titles at the end of the film, which is another insistence which finally broke old habits. That I feel the words come gentler & interfere with vision less, if they occur at the end of the film, even though the people maybe know the title of the film they're going to see. So then I thought—that made me unhappy because then I thought oh shit, once again there's nothing for the projectionist to focus on. So therefore I just left the copyright at the beginning of it as a bracket and the real stuff occurs in the middle.

It seems that your films might be short flashes of light, flashes of mind, inspiration, almost a separate personal eye seeing all these things on the ground, and then how do you structure something like that that seems to almost inherently tend to a short film, how do you structure a long film?

Well, I exhausted everything I know. That's again as to why it's called *The Text of Light*. There are certain number of exten-

sions of light taking place that I have seen. So I exhaust all those
I have seen, within a construction that gives me a sense of the
whole world. And in fact to me on one level the film really can
be seen very much as if exploring an alien planet which is very
similar to the one we live on in many respects. Once I had
exhausted…the ash tray had metaphored for me and I had exhausted all that I had seen elsewhere, then I stopped shooting.
And ordered that like a text, you could almost say an alphabet
from the simple to the more complex, from the horizontal to the
vertical, from meshes of light just come clumping, making tri-
angles of mountain-like shapes through to finally what appears
to me as a whole forest of trees. And that's one level of the film.
Again, it was to structure it in a whole world sense and so there's
also, there's a four season structure to it which cycles again and
again. There's day and night. There's all that I know and all
that's most familiar to me. Then too, that I was very moved by
the symphonic form. I've always believed film is most close to
music of all the other arts. It came quite naturally into four
movements.

You answered it in a sense in what you just mentioned about the sym-
phonic form and I was wondering whether at the start or somewhere
involved in the middle of the film you have any connections to music or
sounds per se because you bring up the scream, etcetera,…& whether
the editing or the pace at which the chops either increase in rapidity or
decrease, give you any kind of musical sense of sound forms.

In terms of the second part of your question, they don't
increase or decrease just like that. There are increases or de-
creases but I can't say that's true as an overall form. But yes I'm
very much involved in music, I listen to music and I mean not
just as a background, but I sit or lie down and listen to it when
I'm home, two or three hours a day. It may be sheerly coinciden-
tal because I don't see any direct ties, but I was very involved in
Schubert's Ninth Symphony while working on this film.

Have you ever associated sounds with color per se?

Yes, there is a melodic line constantly going through all the work as of the last decade. And I do think of shifting changes and tones, in most films a very cordial melodic development; and I'm very concerned with that. That's how I feel film and music are the closest—they share tone. And they're also that close in that they're primarily dependent upon rhythm and tempo. And they're continuity arts and so on. But tone I take as seriously in film reaching toward music as Messiaen does in music reaching toward color.

Why didn't you use music to add to the contemplation in this film?

Well because it would distract and be redundant and cut back seeing. All sound that does occur in sync, or intentional relationship with music, does diminish sight. So I've always thought of it—that you have to pay a price when you use a sound. And there are very few people that estimate that rightly. One of the greatest, *the* greatest in my opinion, is Peter Kubelka, who really knows how difficult it is to make a sound film. You cannot take for granted that you just have a picture and a sound to go with it. Not at all. And I never felt a need for sound. Though I'm not against sound, as my praise of Kubelka and James [Broughton] ought to make clear. And Kenneth Anger, all three of whom work with sound in absolutely magical and incredible ways. But for myself I have moved along the line of the silent film which has a very special discipline; and I do that because of my own necessities to see certain particularities that tend to get blurred if accompanied by sound. Or, I have found no way to keep from damaging by any relationship to sound. On the other hand, I have just finished a 20 minute sound/sync film, the first sync film I ever made. And I'm very excited about it.

I know that your 8mm works, your Songs, *were edited in the camera, and later you were very concerned with the energy you received from…*

Well, no, some were, most weren't. It's always an ideal to edit in the camera, for obvious reasons...I think. The more obvious reasons are to me that there is an energy in the moment of shooting which editing again can leak out for you. What's interesting to me is the energy of immediacy. That comes out of my involvement with Charles Olson. The actual breath and physiology of the living person being present at its most, uninterrupted by afterthought. Editing is always afterthought. Though the way to beat that is to get *that* excited at the editing table. And that's very hard.

But in the case of this film it is very highly edited. And I prefer the word "arranged." And again I think we need a better word. "Arranged" is gentler & reminds me of the composer. "Compose" would be another word. We're talking about a composition in time. To make a construct that will fill completely the length of time it runs. I trust more myself what happens in the immediacy of shooting rather than in this afterthought process.

For Robert Duncan and Jess.

Remarks following a screening of The Text of Light
at the San Francisco Art Institute, November 18, 1974.

poetry and film

The arts, always, when I went through school — and I only went as far as one uncompleted semester at college — the arts were always considered secondary. And the arts are an older discipline than any of these upstarts like science, and cooking; yet cooking is an art in terms of its condition as being an old discipline. So today we are gathered about poetry and film. And I want to say some simple things which are always hard to teach because I have to dig thru a lot of pitchblende to get to the radium.

I think that one of the greatest lessons I ever had in poetry was one night I was invited over to Kenneth Rexroth's house in the early 1950's in San Francisco. Rexroth was one of the two centers of poetic activity in San Francisco at that time. He would send out calls to those who came to his house, and those who would be interested gathered informally in his living room. On this particular night a man from India began to read Tagore in Bengali. Now, I have read a lot of translated Tagore, and I never liked it very much; but now out came these extraordinarily beautiful sounds. First of all I was learning that poetry was not translatable. Second, because this was such a great experience beyond anything I had ever had before, or usually sense in poetry, I realized how important it was to approach poetry first thru its sounds. And then I learned, later, that was a way for some people to approach film first, just through its vision. People who had found difficulties with films of mine and other contemporaries because of their subject matter, like they say, or the lack of it, as some thought, or their dislocation of things in subject matter, could suddenly recognize a beauty, just in the tailoring of the light. They saw that this was more than decoration —or something like a light show—but that it was a very articulate rhythm, that is, it carried the motion. One could feel something about just the qualities of the lights. So the trick for seeing that was to throw the film absolutely out of focus. This film I am going to show you most of you have not seen in any other form. Then you will have a chance to test the theory. After you have seen it out of focus, I will show it to you in focus.

(Shows film)

Once I threw a film by Sergei Eisenstein, *Ivan the Terrible*, completely out of focus, and didn't tell people what it was, but I asked them to state their emotional feelings about certain passages. I did passage by passage. There was quite an accuracy: 80-90% agreed what was a sad passage or an excited one, and even thematic senses of battle between good and evil, black and white. Certainly very simple things, to be sure, but they at least were in agreement that this film out of focus and with no subtitles to read and no sound track to hear caused accurate, what would have been regarded as accurate emotional responses.

So I know there are people, for instance, that if you think of all the trouble people have with the meaning they take Ezra Pound—for example or Allen Ginsberg— to have, then they are just put off from hearing the music; whereas what they hear in a foreign language doesn't prejudice them against the song. They may indeed later decide that the things that have shaped the poet's life bother them in one way or another, but they aren't predisposed against the song. As I understand it that's terribly important, because what we have in the arts is that you may listen to your worst enemy's song.

Now I'm trying to talk about things that are all the same between poetry and film. That it is a meeting ground, as I see it. How many of you have seen Leni Riefenstahl's *Triumph of the Will*? Well, she in my view is a great film artist who, to be sure, made films that Hitler admired, about Hitler that he admired very much, notably *Triumph of the Will*. Jewish organizations, with all their justification, gather and picket the showing of her

works. I think that's a mistake, actually; I think it would be far
smarter if the Jewish organizations arranged wide distribution
of those films for the following reason: because she was an artist, she left us a portrait of that whole time. I wish that the terrifying images which Leni Riefenstahl managed in *Triumph of the
Will* of Hitler—which is really about the Nurenberg rally—I
wish that that was available for people to see because, as an art,
it is not persuasive. The interesting thing about *Triumph of the
Will* is that Hitler thought it was marvelous as a portrait of him,
and, at the same time, the British Propaganda Ministry used
that film to scare Britain into arming. That was the last straw:
they didn't change one word, they didn't misrepresent one thing,
they took the whole thing just as Hitler liked it and Leni Riefenstahl made it and scared the western world half to death with it.
Because it was an art, it changed the capacity for people to see
something. And I have no doubt that most of the people most
of the time will decide against that, so the wide distribution of
Leni Riefenstahl's work would be a benefit in the world; whereas
when people don't decide, everything that Hitler was gets distorted by public education. Gradually the menace he represents
—and to me a terrible menace—falls into a kind of hero worship, the kind that Napolean would get, who was the same kind
of bastard.

So there are grounds that film and poetry and other arts in
various ways share. But film and poetry relate rather closely for
this reason: poetry is dependent upon a language that is in the
air. All poets inherit at scratch a language—I mean they inherit
it the first time they start scratching their ears with sound and
start to make sense out of it, that is, as babies. And they inherit
not only their language, but the possibility of language, which is
a concept which is really incredible. It enables them, for one
thing, to go on to learn other languages. There's something very
solidly there that's not there as an art tradition, but is there as an
everyday tradition. Then poets are forever surrounded by other

people using this language and using it all the time in a great variety of ways, which shapes each poet's sense of that language. And then—and here's the miracle—they override that constant mundane chit-chat of people that's not actually much different than monkeys. Just chit-chatting and passing clichés, comfort and admonition, back and forth. The five messages of people which aren't much different from what Hollis Frampton defined as the five bird songs. Birds, he says, have about five things to say. As Hollis has it with the birds they say "good morning," "I found a worm," "love me," "get out," "good night." Now a great deal could be done with that, which is the ordinary business of the world and a great variety of song can be made of that for those that really listen to the little varieties of generalized bird songs; and therein to the little varieties, if you really get ears that keen, to listen to particular birds of the species. In their own language all those varieties which I love too, all those words, aside from those I just spoke, that fill up the *Oxford English Dictionary*, plus all the words that have been hatched since then. So look at the *OED* and think about what actually has to be said, and see the wonderful variety of possibilities within, particularly, our language, for shades of meaning, or for music. To me, all the rest is noise. That gets quite personal. What's regarded by others as noise your own true love makes as music. Then there is music that overrides just that personal, which is to say, that a noise that some poet makes becomes music to several who care so much about it they will risk their lives to save it for anybody who wants it.

For example, the great moment of this to me in history is when some monks unwrapping paupers' coffins found shards of Greek poetry. For pauper graves they didn't use wood, they took old manuscripts, old books and pulped them, and made little paper coffins for the poor. Some of those were unearthed, and among the papers were found shards of Greek poetry and it was determined from some of the saved poems that these were shards of Sappho, and others. These monks with great excitement sent this news to the Pope. Meanwhile they were slowly pulling apart these coffins to get more and more little shards of poetry. It took a long time, thank God, for news to get around in those days, so by the time the Pope got the message and had determined on it and sent back his determination, these monks were very involved in this poetry and were loving it, loving it enough to keep at this tedious task of slowly unraveling it from a mass of decay. The Pope announced that this was pagan poetry and was to be destroyed. We have to assume for most of the monks that that was the word of God. But they so loved the poetry by that time that they disregarded it, which meant not only that they were willing to die for it, but risk their immortal souls to save the poetry. That's how we have the better part of Sappho that we still have. It doesn't take very many people to save something, but it takes an incredible passion.

Well, I think it starts with a rhythm, it starts with a recognizable rhythm, a rhythm that moves past all the clichés of language. Someone learns to so order these mundane words of chit-chat that they make a rhythm of them which is compelling. One good way to get a sense of what poetry is at its greatest is to get some records of poetry in other languages that you do not understand and listen to the music of them. I don't mean to stop there, I don't mean that poetry is without meaning. That would be sound and fury signifying nothing. But I mean, put the horse before the cart, start with the compelling rhythm that someone lifts from all the chit-chat which is a buzz, a noise or an annoyance to most of us, unless we get our message for the day—do this do that—or hello or I love you, or pass the cereal. Get past that and see that someone was compelled to lift those chunks into a meaningful rhythm. That's what I hope to achieve by showing the film totally out of focus. Now I would like to show you the film in focus and then maybe we can talk about means and meaning.

(Shows film: Two:Creeley/McClure*)*

Let me ask if any of you have questions.

Do you have any idea of poetry when you work on films?

Yes, though differently in all cases. I had definitely in mind to get a portrait of Robert Creeley when we visited him in Placitas, New Mexico, in 1962. With Michael we were leaving San Francisco and I had never taken any images of him. I had, oh, maybe 50 feet in the camera. And I said let me get some pictures of you, and instantly I took the first little bit I suddenly knew that I wanted more than just some pictures of him. That whole section on Michael McClure has no editing — I knew suddenly I had to do something and it took all morning. He very graciously sat down and I got out the image of him with the lion make-up on *Ghost Tantras* — with the hair all over his face — and interspersed images of that with images of him sitting there in the chair, and he meantime was doing certain things as he sat and I was waiting and we were also talking, about Milton, as I recall. Even though that started just to get some pictures of him, very instantly as I started photographing it turned into a portrait. In the case of the film *Hymn to Her* I was just shooting some film, in that case of Jane, as I do around the house, and it fell later into this portraiture.

Do you concentrate in the camera or on the printing?

Both, whatever is necessary. Preferably in the camera be-cause it's cheaper. It also has a higher energy level usually. It's less interfered with—it just has the vibrancy of immediacy that's hard, very much harder to get later, editing or printing.

Was that film Two:Creeley/McClure...

That was definitely solarized, that is, by having a negative made, and then an A&B roll, and solarizing.

How did you get the shimmering effect on the tree in the film The Wold Shadow *you showed last night?*

Single framing.

It looked like colors running up the tree at one point.

Well, that's painting on glass. The pane of glass sits on an easel between me and the scene. I take a frame and alter what I'm seeing by painting on that glass and taking another frame, etc.

But these things don't happen that way. I don't say, oh, today I'll go and take a piece of glass into the woods and see what hanky-panky I can produce. But quite the reverse. I had an experience at that spot in the woods which did never recur, though I waited for months. A large anthropomorphic shadow appeared over me in the trees; and if I'd been a sensible, so-called primitive person I would have fallen to my knees or run like hell. First, when I saw it, I said, that's interesting how that shadow is made by the light. It gradually dawned on me as I tried to figure out what was throwing that shadow that there wasn't anything, that the light was not so positioned in any way that I could account for that shadow, which then seemed *very* awesome and frightening. I just stood with my mouth open in amazement. Then the shadow faded back into the trees. I presumed that I had seen the god of the forest, or of that place. I went back every day to worship, but that god wasn't up for religion, because he never came again. I did the next best thing to either falling on my knees or running like hell. I went back to that place with the idea in mind to paint the shadow as I had seen it, but better — as I started making the film — I let that go and made an *homage* to that place, an *homage* to that god or goddess, not just out of some kindliness of my heart but so I could sleep easily at night that I had done my bit in the great dance with mystery. And fortunately instead of doing that stupid thing I thought I was going to do, paint the god that no longer reappeared, I made a full exposition of everything of that place that I felt, and I reflected as I sat there painting all those things that Eastman Kodak's film does not usually accommodate. I can't put a camera inside my head to photograph my own optic system as it is seeing, so I have to paint. As I went on painting all day—the day passed slowly—to take a frame and then paint and then take another frame 24 times to make a second of film is a full day's hard labor to get 100 feet thru the camera. And then as I went on painting, all such places came rich in my mind, all such places as the history of painting has brought them to us. The word "wold" is there because if you look in the *OED*, it is a wood. Originally it was a wood and then it came to mean a flat place, and then again a wood. Along hundreds of years of the English language, and directly because of the acts of the poets, the word got shifted to mean these alternative things. We now have "wold" as the source of the word "wood." But so all these dreams tumbled thru my head, of language and painting and feeling about that place. The fact is that on one level the film is a whole history of landscape painting right up to an *homage* to someone like Clyfford Still, who is really a landscape painter. And that's how I make films; and that's a very normal process, as far as the arts are concerned.

Your comments on why you use the painting in that film relate to the comments you made last night, and that made me wonder if you ever investigated Kirlian photography.

Yes, Kirlian photography has been very helpful to me because I have seen many of those things, just with my eyes, for years, and when I spoke of them was called quite mad. Many of the reasons I paint on film is to get an approximation of some of the things that are now photographable thru the Kirlian process. So Kirlian photography came along and established that my seeing was not mad. But note the despair of the times in which we live. Because a machine can see it, it's now considered sane. Now I can speak of it as halos that surround plants and fingers and heads, and if people look skeptical I can say I'm into Kirlian photography.

I'm also very grateful for reading some other human's equivalent to something I'm seeing. Much that Wilhelm Reich has seen I had seen before I read him. And in ways sufficiently the same and also different; his writing was a comfort at one point, because it was the only feedback I had. It was a comfort that another human being had also seen some of the things. This is entirely aside from what the orgone box might be. I don't know anything about that. I tend not to be interested in it. But what he wrote about having seen, much of it I have seen in various ways.

We're now talking about means, but not about meaning. Let me tell you this story. When I was going through school I was always carrying a poetry book—I was very interested in poetry and still am—and so I got a bad reputation as a kid carrying books when he didn't have to. When I had my sixteenth birthday party, a bunch of my friends as a joke got together—well first of all they were going to buy me a birthday present—and what else but a book. While they were downtown looking for a present, they found something that would be a hilarious joke. They found a book that was so absurd and ridiculous and impossible that even I would be defeated at trying to read it. They were doubling over with laughter at the thought of giving me *this book* that would truly defeat me. And sure enough came this book all wrapped in tissue paper, and I was delighted because I loved books and they were sensible enough to give me a book; and I opened the paper and there was a very strange book indeed. First of all it seemed to be in English, but at least a third of it was in other languages; and it made references to the gods. Just to get thru some of the courses at school I can remember writing on my arm in indelible ink, Mercury, Zeus, Jupiter and having little definitions of what all these were. It annoyed me to have references to a whole pack of gods from elsewhere; the final incredible thing was that this gift book was filled with Chinese. This of course was Ezra Pound's *Cantos,* which is, if I must choose one book, the single most important book in my life. Indeed I couldn't read it and they had their good laugh. I could only put together three words in a row and then stumble over a lot I couldn't understand and then three more words that I could understand. But right off the bat, because I was too desperate not to be defeated in the teeth of my friends who were getting too much of a laugh out of this, I started the book and it starts "And then went down to the ship." Right there [*writes on board*] I noticed something: "And." To start off a book like this with "and"! I am very concerned with the beginning and endings of books—"and"—that was thrilling. And immediately it moved all the emotions this way [*writes on board* →]—so powerful. I remember it brought tears to my eyes, which no doubt increased the laughter of my friends. And the next word which hit me was "down," "and then went *down*." "Set forth" was there too. And within those lines you also get "up." In those first two lines the mind splits, the mind moving, going in two directions and very powerfully and very reinforced. That kind of thing is where the relationship between my sense of poetry and what film can do begins, and that is like the first level set of meaning: direction! The poem has the capacity beyond just its rhythm to make reference to the process of thinking itself. If you set that in a model —that's forward and back. Poetry is having to do with the actual process of thought, as absolutely distinct from what I don't regard as poetry at all, the writer telling you his mind, or something of that sort. It certainly *seems* like Ezra Pound is primarily involved with telling his mind; you know, he's telling what he thinks is good and what he thinks is bad, but I hear his song, and I heard it even when I was utterly baffled by a book that obviously had been given to me as a joke. It wasn't just my stubbornness, and I had certainly encountered other books that were tough and tougher to read than that; but after comprehending something of them I threw them out. Here was one that the more I understood the more yield came to me. So here became the great book for going over and over and over. Now I would say that I can read six to ten, in some places twenty words in a row, which isn't very much still, but it's good progress in a life time's worth of reading. I'm working on it. I've got some of the major slogans that were to sustain me all of my life, prayers, like "All that is is light." That is enough to return me to that kind of person Pound is who would know how important it is to say and give Erigena a translation — "All that is is light." It's so powerful in that context. That's something of what I mean by meaning. And **I'M TOUGH ABOUT IT**.

I'd like to talk about direction as circle, as in *A ROSE IS A ROSE IS A ROSE IS A* .

That's the way Gertrude Stein originally wrote in a child's book called *The World Is Round*. It's first written this way because Rose, the little heroine, carves it in a tree. I think it arose that simply in Gertrude's life, because very shortly she was using it on her stationery. But suddenly Gertrude had the sense that she had been given a great gift. First of all it's a wonderful center-piece of arguments for her great teacher, William James, about the nature of being and nothingness before it got obfuscated into that, in my opinion, by the existentialists. It looks like a silly thing—ok, we got it—a rose is a rose is a rose. It means it is only and ever a rose. That's something to brood on, and we could say that's kind of a silly poem. After it sprang from her subconscious mind into this child's book, she must have come to realize the incredible puns that move through it. There is a reference that she was aware of those, though she wouldn't be as academic as I am to lay it all out here. Someone was once attacking the poem in Chicago, and she said "all I have to say is that the rose has not bloomed so sweetly in English poetry in 200 years." Which meant that she had come to recognize what that whole tradition of English poetry is; so poetry always has a tradition, a whole lattice of meaning. So the rose, if having looked at the whole history of English poetry as a history, is used in three basic symbol places: birth, sex, death. (AROSE) Here we have a nice pun for birth, for something coming up; here we have his Eros, sex; and with a slight slur, we can get sorrows; with another slight slur we can get the connective, the thing that relates symbolically, arrows. What springs magically if you start feeling it with the tongue, as distinct from just taking it along with the clichés of everyday language, birth, sex, death is represented back thru the Greek, and perhaps earlier, by the three sisters. The three sisters are in there. She glorified that sense of the forest by laying it out in a line, not always putting it in a circle. So it's a meditation piece as a poem which has to do certainly with the whole history of English toying with these particular words, and these qualities of meaning. There are other kinds of spring-off from it, like for an English garden, that is planted in *rows*. But some of this begins to stretch; but those stretches are important too. To read a poem to its outer limits, or a single line, to take the stretches and know they are stretches of meaning but let the stretches go until they snap at you.

Speaking of the sense of meaning that is sometimes in the air around, in the film that you've seen, *Two: Creeley/McClure*, the rhythmic song of being out of focus, as if it were in another language, and then seen again straight thru, and having talked a great deal about the means of how such things are made, I'd like to emphasize that just like Gertrude stumbled into means so I stumbled into those means or am forced to them. I didn't certainly go out of my way to do A and B rolls, because it's just hell. So, I'm driven to it.

Well, then you say this film is a portrait; what does it have to do with Robert Creeley or Michael McClure? Michael McClure when he reads his poetry, he often reads especially softly the capitalized letters. Now he may have changed his act these days, but in the past that was a shock to people because Michael uses a lot of capitalized whole lines. Everyone expects when you see capitalized, that means headlines, that means *WAR IS DE-CLARED!* No—he reads them softer than the rest. He reads slowly, and he moves slowly. But his section in the film is the flashy one with a lot of single framing and quick movements, and there is quite a variety of rhythms in there. Unless you're really up to looking at rhythms fast right off, it just looks like all flickering and burning, whereas Michael tends to move very stately. But I saw him as a man containing an electricity that is just terrifying. It can be deceptive. Everyone says he is so in control, but really he *has* to be, because he is so nervous. He is such a bag of nerves that if he lets himself go he might just go up in smoke. And this manifests itself to the careful looker thru the slightest of ticks or ripples along his skin or in his voice. To the slightest shift of means and meaning. And it is all there in his poetry.

Also you come to who's doing the viewing. Marvell's view of a coy mistress is not going to satisfy a women's libber of then or now. So when someone writes a poem about someone, the primary thing one is learning about is the poet and what he or she thinks, and the rhythm of the self it carries. And the other thing becomes the lumen. Well, people call me subjective because I insist that I am I. There is this argument against my work which says that the film is all me, it's enclosed but it doesn't communicate, doesn't have anything to do with social values, other people can't understand it, and so on. And I make my case as the following. If they are right, if a documentary indeed has to be made as if I have in mind an audience of six-year-old adults being spoon-fed the right idea—if that's documentary, or represents the truth, or any kind of a full circle, well then the newspapers do best represent truth, because that's their bright idea. How many of you have had any kind of newspaper write about you? Did you think the article represented truth? It's the most available source of such undercurrent parlance that we have. A color-blind reporter at an art show would obviously do better than an editor writing the story in the office, particularly if he knew his credentials. He could say, this is what I saw. This is the first level of truth; but the other is, if it goes into the lattice which the arts represent, if it's in relationship to a history or a tradition, then we have the possibility that the tradition can be learned sufficiently to read that thing, be it in paint or along the line of notes in the air or poetry or film—to have a world that passed thru one another human being that's up there spinning, so to speak. That's obviously a world as when Michelangelo saw people beginning to worship the Pieta, what did he do?—a beautiful artist's thing kicking in the teeth of the whole Renaissance as he did so—he carved across the breast band of the Virgin: "Made by Michelangelo." It was more outrageous than a factory worker writing "Made in Tokyo" across his work.

The anecdote comes from Charles Olson—"There is no such many as mass." Which is an incontrovertible truth, or a simpler way to get it is to go out on the street and ask people "are you the average man or woman," and some will say yes, because they've been taught to do so, and then ask them how they've come to think they are. Poets know this, filmmakers know this, and it isn't a case of my using the "I" egocentrically, as so much as Robert Duncan, another poet, puts it: "I" must never arise in the poem except as the communal "I." That's where we come to means and meaning. I know *Two: Creeley/ McClure* is a film and I wish to make a world which is built out of what has passed thru my experience of those two fine men. And to approach each of them with all that I have of my experience of each of them. In both cases it happened to involve much more time spent reading their poetry than sitting around talking with them. I know it's me reading poetry—it isn't a Great Books compendium survey of how people read Michael McClure or Robert Creeley, it's my reading of them that's informed my life. Who else can I speak for? And that shapes the rhythm of which these films are compounded; along with, and in a dance with each of them, which in many ways is contradictory, the poetry rhythms actually on the page, unless you look closer. In Michael's case it would appear to be very stately and very composed. But right under the skin surface ripple constantly impulses that are visible if you choose to look for them, however hard he builds his muscles at Vic Tanney's gym and holds himself in, firm. All the firmness, as of my being a filmmaker as distinct from a poet, has to do with centered weakness. He must be strong, he must be composed, he must be almost statuesque at times to contain this fire that moves thru him. He expressed it in one statement he gave me in the '60s—as we used to call to each other in desperation across the yawning void—"Be a solid moving thru an Inferno." That has to do with the flickering side of him. In relationship to Creeley—those who know Creeley—well, he's a man who didn't come to full sentences until he was 11 or 12 years old, and he stumbles into speech with great hesitancy and enormous power and fantastic delicacy. He's New Englandish; shy, he's incredibly shy. Bob seems like one of those people born old—an old soul you could say. And I saw him that way. Also, he commands a kind of attention where the eyes can become saturated, so engaged and reaching out to help him to come to speech that you get a reverse action. I'm sure all of you are aware if you watch a light bulb that actually at some point, if you're relaxed, that light bulb can be impressing the optic nerve so much that it turns black. Closing the eyes will leave a blue light bulb, usually, drifting off into the void, which is a reversal color of yellow. In the will to give out, it has to be relaxed, at least in my experience; a person can shift from positive to negative. That is, the values can reverse, the eyes are saturated and go to the opposite. So I'm always in that sense after equivalents of things I've seen. My experience isn't exactly like it appears on film, but it's an equivalent. And this reversal of light-value vision happens very often to me when I'm with Robert Creeley. So it seems necessary in the film to seem true to my experience of him.

What you've said about the film has already helped my appreciation of it. Have you ever done program notes, or does that go against your purpose?

I think there are ways to talk about all the arts. I'm here talking but, finally, the world is really *attacking* its contemporary arts with language, largely. I think one of the signs of the greatness of Dante's *Divine Comedy* is that it has survived hundreds and hundreds of years of footnotes. All that attack against the essential ingredient, which is a celebration of mystery! That doesn't mean a lack of mystery. Celebration of mystery allows the maker to acknowledge, by the way he or she has done something, that he or she knows something. But this knowledge also acknowledges mysteries. And the work reverberates. And the mysteries open up further knowing. Now, Robert Frost is a perfect example of someone who just writes a mystery. He writes poems which do celebrate mystery and in the second stage, when you see that he understands something of the mystery, it still can reverberate a little further. But for me it didn't reverberate any further than that. So he is a kind of a nostalgia. I deeply appreciate what he gave me. He's a simple-minded poet, which is OK. It isn't that he lacks intellect. A real simpleminded poet is Christopher Smart, but "My Cat Jeffrey" keeps yielding more and more as I read it across the years, as distinct from "The Road Not Taken." At some point the road not taken is completely taken. There are nursery rhymes that have lasted better. That's what I've called a weak impulse, but there are people one outgrows, or moves away from. It would be nice to think there will be a senile old age when Robert Frost will be just the thing. That is not a put-down. It will be an enormous relief to think that when I get older and get simpleminded I and Frost and nursery rhymes can survive all the same. But in the meantime Ezra Pound is the sustaining one, the one I still can't understand. But at every stage of gained knowledge *The Cantos* reveal more and more to me. They may be rummaged for further understanding he is opening up to me: the Chinese dictionary, which I have now been studying for several years, The *Egyptian Book of the Dead*. Pound probably wouldn't have approved of the *Egyp-*

tian Book of the Dead, but that Dover edition with the way to study the ideograms came along, and I've been studying it. Pound goads me on because at each turn in the reading of him I come to new mysteries which he has set significantly within learned reach.

Again, your appreciation of Pound has come from reading the poems again and again, as well as the materials around the poems. For us to appreciate films more, have you ever thought of writing program notes?

I've written several books. *Metaphors on Vision* which is considered the most difficult book on film to read. I also consider it as such. I think it's worthily difficult, but I wish it could have been simpler, like *The Brakhage Lectures.* One of the nicest books I wrote is *The Moving Picture Giving and Taking Book*, or *Seen.* I've written a lot and I make a living talking about films, and I'm also aware and would warn you, that the only value in this lecturing to make a living decently, is that we see how works withstand this honest verbal outpouring. We see that despite all this talk they still stand there, withstand the investigation. I don't really trust doctors, certainly not surgeons. I think the great thing about going to the hospital and having surgery is to survive it. To survive this probing, the operation called education, is really my sense of it. Then I see the colleges as a vast salmon run with most students flopping on the rocks at the side and some few despite the downpour making it up stream to spawn. I think it is a more severe survival testing grounds than the U.S. Marines.

What would be the point to all these lectures. Finally I hope to take a silly little poem like "Rose is a rose is a rose" and ask that question in Grand Forks, North Dakota, and in New York City, where almost anyone's heard it, and chuckled over it and then dismissed it. But at least for whatever it's worth, it's one poem that's in the language and known by more people probably than any other poem in the world. And there is a lesson in that. If you start breaking it down, you see that that little tiny bit contains, from my viewpoint, an infinite amount of meditative possibilities. It keeps being alive and rolling around and round in my head and yielding more and more. All of which is to say that film does not have a chance equal to a poem in our time, because there is no way I can pass out to those of you who are interested *Two: Creeley/McClure* to take it home and run it to death or into a lifetime's viewing. I've written a lot, I've spoken a lot, I've tried to make talk into as much integrity as possible.

[1977]

recent
writings

Short Films 1975

gertrude stein:
meditative literature and film

Metaphor can be said to have been born as an evasion of "straight talk" or what's known as The Simple Truth.

It can also, as such, be said to have come into Human Consciousness in order to resolve Dualities.

("The Simple Truth" is bound to be a lie, considering the complex nature of Being.

Thus Humans evolved puns and all multiple levels of The Paradoxical, or a way to get at Complex Truth.)

In either case, the Western emphasis of/on Metaphor is clearly one of Transformation.

As such it can be thought of as a passage and ritualized through either story-telling or meditation.

There are only five stories, epitomized by filmmaker Hollis Frampton thinking of the five bird songs:

(1) Good Morning.
(2) I found a worm.
(3) Love me.
(4) Get out.
(5) Good Night.

Literary *Meditation* offers greater possibilities and is known in Prose as either Reflection or Description.

All writers who eschew story *altogether* are essential aspiring to the philosophical.

Literary description is essentially futile to the extent that is attempts to fill in the spaces between named-shapes.

Description is, on average, a thousand words *trying* to be a Picture.

This essay is dedicated to Marilyn Jull Brakhage: it could not have existed without her careful questioning of every premise. *[1990]*

But with Moving Pictures we have, finally, the possibility of moving visual thinking

— a thousand words every 1/48th-of-a-second and, as the mind moves, a corollary of Philosophy.

Words, at best then, could be left free for reflection and signification

— free from lists, and The Symbolic, to become Signs along routes of Passage to the origin of language

...which has been the center of modernistic literary concern in our Time

(much as Paint, freed by The Photograph from representation, has reverted to its glyphic roots).

Gertrude Stein sensed paint and writ as freed from an obligation to re-present.1

She moved to allow her writing to exist as Presence, to be a present to the reader.

She defined The Reader as 'herself and strangers,' presumably because one cannot *easily* image communicating with strangers...or at all with oneself.

One reads "between the lines," with Gertrude Stein, to get whatever sense of "message" available

...which is, therefore, carried primarily by rhythm, textures-of-sound, and reference conjunction:

"As a Wife has a Cow a Love Story," can be parsed sexually through the varieties-of-insistence of just those words

— the aspirants and exhalations bracketing "Wife" opening into various vowel "o"s

— the oddity of "Cow" in the referential context, the disjunction of cliche thus

...this the more natural route to understanding of the poem, or even its title, than the imaginably logical "Wife has pet Cow, loves it," of "My wife Has a Cow and I Love Her."

When she writes "I am I because my little dog knows me," the sound palindrome "I am I" bespeaks integrity-of-being

...“I am I be-” breaks “I” empathetically into “cause” — breaks “I am”/”I be-” alphabetically.

...“my” introduces, possessively, “li” of “little,” running on rhythmically appropriate “feet” of “dog”

—whose “aw” puns “knowledge” of “me” with “nose,” and “n” “o”s—all of which is a resounding **NO** to Descartes’ “I think, therefore I am.”

When she seems to simply name (or noun), over and over again, the puns take over emphatically:

The clarity of the poem suggests full-face-shape of the flower, the syllables the petals.

The “o”s rhyme this shape in sound, the *sisses* the three sisters of Fate: Birth, Sex, Death.

Birth is to be found, past tense, as growth, by slurring “a rose,” or by dropping the “s” for “ro(e)”…egg of fish (symbolic origin of life).

Though this work of Stein’s is most usually invoked as a joke, it is, nevertheless, the most oft’ quoted poem in the English language.

It is a demonstration of the utter other-worldliness of language constructs—the rrrr-0-sis/buzz print-and-paper ROSE is.

And yet, within the interlock of sound puns, there is no more brief exactitude of descript-meaning yet attained on the subject.

Thus this wheel of Stein’s rolls on through the minds of stranger multitudes, its means intact despite multitudinous usage

...precisely because it is not didactic: it is, rather, a construct integral with itself, a paradigm as such.

Ulla Dydo has finally made a study of the Yale Stein collection sufficient to explicate Stein's work process, thus:

"...two kinds of Stein manuscripts. The first, for which I use the French name *carnets*...consists of preliminary notes and partial jottings...most *carnets* are small pocket note-books, but scraps of paper also appear.

"The second are the manuscript notebooks proper, or *cahiers*...in these are the Stein texts and any revisions. Many texts were composed directly in the *cahiers*, but others were partly or completely copies."

The *carnets*, which include "shopping lists, addresses, guest lists," as well as private love poems to Alice, tend to constitute *source* of her work in daily life.

The *cahiers* are often, then, translations of daily privacies into corroborative texts

...texts charged with the energies of personal immediacy and the unfettered passion of the private

...texts translated into the textures and textually-tempered rhythmically lettered orders of Literature

—a construct of words integral each with each other, and integrally "true to" each other's formal order in paradigmatically being together.

It is not necessary, or even useful, for the reader to know that "cow" is Gertrude's baby-talk for "orgasm"

...that "tender buttons" are Alice's nipples: these energies have been metamorphosed into that which is available to The Reader.

The Reader/"stranger" who, presumably, has his/her own personal love life to live...free of Alice B. Toklas altogether.

When yearning for Fame was to overwhelm Gertrude Stein, she reversed her poetic tactics and wrote *The Autobiography of Alice B. Toklas.*

In the early years of my adult living this book and her *Three*

Lives, *Ida* and *The Making of Americans* dominantly influenced my work.

I understood the qualities of Dailiness in her first works and her final writings, the playfulness of her dramas and rhetoric.

And when I didn't understand I quoted her explanations, or those of Donald Sutherland, or simply parroted "well, my dear, what's the question?"

She inspired much daily flimmaking of mine, a whole oeuvre of autobiographical cinematography in non-repetitive variations.

But I then was, as was she, infected with Drama as an assumption; and assumptions always pre-suppose some sense of repetition.

In 1932, as Stein toiled with the more literal *Autobiography of Alice B. Toklas*, she also composed her epic poem "Stanzas in Meditation."

This work, more than any other, has inspired most of my filmmakmg, and almost all of my aesthetics, the last half-decade or so.

The poem, one of the few completed epics of our century, begins:

"I caught a bird which made a ball."

(Each word already seems—once the conjunction of "bird" and "ball" reverberates—to have a life of its own.

...the vowels "I - a- a - i - i - a - a - a" rub off-rhymes against each other: "I - aw - a - er - ih - a - a - aw"

the "caught"/"ball" rhyme is offset by the "I-bird-which," twists of "i"-vowel in a, thus, disjunct run of "a"s.)

The second line disrupts whatever connective logic one attempts:

"And they thought better of it."

(Beginning with an "aaa" as out-of-tune with a run-of-"a"s as bugle blast, the "they" then "a"-rhymes; "thought"'s "aw" "caught" /"ball"..."of" "*it*"?

"...thought better of it" is a whole cliche smashed to pieces under the weight of "it," making no more sensible reference than as off-rhyme to "which"

..."they," thus, begins its life as a character in the poem, giving life to "which," to "a" with its shades-of-pronunciation, to "aw," so on.)

Ideas arise in the poem (the "caught-bird-ball" as an art form, say, or the "they" as the "thought"— judges of it):

but words are no more serving the collective rhetoric or thoughts of the author than they are, each, characterizing each-and-every word's evolution in the course of the poem.

But a poem is not a film; (and prose is even a less likely corollary to a moving imagery art).

For it is in the nature of Image that it is received as a clustering of object-shapes to be individually perceived

Viewers of imagery are, therefore, less visually subservient in reception than readers who are, after all, strung along a line-of-words

unless, that is, the viewer be hypnotized into passivity by compartmentally rigged compositions of easily nameable cliches

—in which case (the average movie-going case) the viewer is even more passive; for the reader must at least imagine what he's read he sees.

Film, if it is to be comparable to Literature, must, first, disrupt every literarily logical assumption that Picture is only a container for the variably nameable

...(only a container carrying all the references along at the same speed/tempo in the identical rhythmic compartmentalization — like, say, a word-furniture van).

Just as Gertrude Stein had to defeat the traditions of descriptive writing, so too must Film free itself from descriptive or referential limitations.

Film must eschew any easily recognizable reference; for reference is always and only achieved along-a-line of Symbolized Signs.

It must give up *all* that which is static, so that even its stillnesses-of-image are ordered on an edge of potential movement.

It must give-over all senses-of-repetitions precisely because Film's illusion-of-movement is based on shot-series of flickering *near*-likenesses of image.

Gertrude Stein has taught me, from scratch, that there is no such imaginable entity as an exactitude of repetition.

There is only a lack-of-attention of a reader, say, hypnotized by language, a spell which makes repetition seem to be so

or sloppiness-of-writing, a whole tradition of such, which Stein was up-against with her: "Let me recite what History teaches. History teaches."

— or —

"Before the flowers of friendship faded friendship faded."

— or —

"Rose is a rose is a rose"...so forth.

"This book is really about the aesthetics of near repetition," as Bruce Kawin says of his *Telling it Again and Again*, on Stein.

The film corollary would not be to show any give "it" or Pic. again and again, but to arrange similar shots to resist any sense of visual recurrence.

Motion Pictures, dominated by narrative dramatic, word-ordered (thus referential) signification inherited, thus, the same problem Gertrude Stein had as writer.

It was enough-too-much of a 'once and future' thing to drive this aesthetically oriented filmmaker to extremes of unutterable abstraction.

And if a work be abstract—i.e. a "take *from*"—**WHAT**

possible tactic could energize what would otherwise be decorative imagery with recognizable feeling?

And if a film be, rather, illustrative—a series of pictures of nameable forms—WHAT on earth might alleviate the inaesthetic burden of referential nomenclature?

My answer is (as inspired by hers) a freeing of each image (as her each-and-every word) to its un-owned self-life within the continuities (rather than context) of the work.

My working process (as illuminated by Dydo's study of Stein's) is to transmogrify (as Stein translates) each vibrancy of unutterably private source into Form.

The forms within The Film will answer only to each other and the form of the paradigm the entirety-of-forms finally is.

And this will axiomatically constitute a meditative art, just as hers is literarily thus, inasmuch as integrity-of-form forms Form.

One can empathize with Hero or Heroine of a narrative-dramatic work, but only at the expense of one's self-awareness and/or meditation on Other.

One can "read" a film along-a-line of names; but *only* at the cost of formal integrity and of meditative *inner* formation.

I have made my *Visions in Meditation* in homage to Gertrude Stein's whole meditative oeuvre epitomized by her "Stanzas in Meditation."

When this series opens with an image of a white building "whited out," it is not necessary to know the source of this photograph.

That the structure represented (and over-exposed) is the oldest church in Maine is not relevant information with respect to the film.

What it referentially is, was (when photographed) crucial to my composing of it, my f-stop "take" of it, the rhythms of my gradual overexposure and, later, editorial juxtaposition of it.

These formal transformations, of this once-church, now exist in a film that will realize itself through the life of shapes of white.

The original cluster-of-shapes generated by this photographed church ought to cause (through shape shifts throughout) some sense of The Sacred.

Each viewer, left free of *my* church-as-such ought to be able to build each his/her cathedral of the imagination free of architecture altogether.

And if not, then, the integrity of these shapes and orders-of-color—each shape and tone having a life of its own — could authenticate also some other level of metaphorical meaning intrinsic to the work

...could even inculcate The Antithetical inasmuch as Art, like Freud's Unconscious, joins opposites as ONE, at once, in Timeless fusion

—though, unlike anything else, each artwork ideally exists as a paradigm which, *fully* meditated-upon, would present the fullest exactitude of meaning imaginable.

It is simply a complex spiritual matter of author *and* reader, or filmmaker and viewer, being true to Source and the fiction of Form at one and the same time.

Let explanation—that after-birth of dramatic assumption —give way to the complex truths of the Transformative.

"Keep it moving," like they say, and/or "Shoot first, and ask questions later," as poet Ed Dorn puts it.

Ulla Dydo is completing *The Language That Rises*, about the ten years of elucidating writing that led up to Gertrude Stein's "Stanzas in Meditation."

She tells me that in a 1913 manuscript of "Sacred Emily" (where the phrase "rose is a rose" is first used) Stein drew a picture, ephemerally suggesting petals, but:

...it is a picture of a cauliflower so perceived as to epitomize, in a way no rose could, the ultimate essence of Rose.

Nightmare Series

manifesto

Hard Times now here!

Wage enslavement nearly complete!

Children essentially raised by The State...wide world over...

(nowhere to run)

A darkening of The Ages has begun...again...

The Arts manifest as mock of what, once, they were.

COMES FILM!, in such a Time, stepchild of Song and Light, twisted out of its natural measure, boxed for cheap narrative dramatic pleasure, stapled, as if forever to Literature, every film little more than a book illustration.

Filmmakers DISunite!—

Protect *independence* against all else!—

Embrace such Dark as The Light has given—

(Films: "Electric Shadows" The Chinese have named Them)—

Every 1/48th-of-a-second turn of projector shutter, each lens-caught bruise of shadow-shape on light-burnt silver halides, each smudge a filmmaker puts upon filmstrip, is interference with the flickering window-of-white Film IS, is projective hubris-of-form interruptive of purest incandescence, IS, as such (to extent one is filmmaker-independent) a wrestle with angels at the foot of Jacob's ladder: ONLY in a six-ways/side-wise balance of Aesthetics could once come, humble, to *this:*

(1) The blackest projected film-leader appears on screen as a softened rectangle of merest glimmer, enhaloed in every eye which perceives it, an ephemeral tracery of the electrified gate from which it is sprung at each twist of shutter, an eerie aerial luminous gel in the mind of each viewer.

(2) Thus, LIGHT can *never*, in this medium, be entirely shadowed-over or referentially defeated (however deflected by literary reference or pictorial obliquity).

(3) Therefore, all honestly independent filmmakers are, as are seers of yore, devotees of Light, and as such inevitably, will-lessly, *will* make whatever each his or her marks upon Film in service to the infinite varieties of recognitions of an reverences for The Light.

(4) Wherefore one comes in time, even such Times as these, to certitude that this medium, Film, *is*, as eyes have it, *at one* with the synapting Human nervous System in evolution...

(5) Inasmuch as, ontologically speaking, all lightning-like Thought had, by the turn-of-the-century, run out of transformative words, run aground "the ineffable," run Dada, soforth...inasmuch as The Mathematical, and all other linearly frozen Symbol, including "the pictorial," had served to separate human animal cells from natural cathexis whereby one knows oneself as light-like (wave particulate) thus like unto The Light...inasmuch as, thus, the simulated movement of *light us thought* had become, as Film, an invention out of absolute necessity, to exteriorize moving visual thinking (much as once the exteriorization of the heartbeat was invented using chest or hollow log for drum).

(6) And theretofore, as filmmaker Len Lye was first to consciously articulate, the mind's eyes, and the cells of the optimal system synapting, most naturally must be prime shaper of the development of Filmic Aesthetics and all corollary Techne (whatever the pleasurable escapist and propagandistic usages commercial/governmental film imposed upon the medium...)

FILM!: that given necessity, first time in Human History, permitting shared thought process...the moves of The Mind, hence that crucial recognition of what we all do *really* share — the lovely though lonely grandeur of every Being's each instant's absolute, and obvious, uniqueness sharable only as we are informed by Lights irreducible biologic synthesis in us.

The commercial cinema fails agains and again, recovers its losses, stumbles on, "looks good" a while, fails once more,

forevermore...for its usages of Film (escapism, a necessity for
wage slaves who cannot plot actual escape except by enslaving
others, "dreams" dreamt-as-manufactured to pass insomniac
nights, unholy orderings for those who fear ordinary chaos,
styles-of-Time for times at status-quo lacking style-as-soul), all
these star-studded pleasurable blasphemies against Film Form,
all The Movies, as they are known in endless merry-go-round,
are norm of encaved humans at play in the imaginary fields of
the social world...no harm in the long run.

But the young, always THE YOUNG, filmmakers devoted to
Art, or otherwise courting The Sacred — that radiance which
sur-rounds each organic cell and is at ONE with The Sun — do
eschew all pretence of social order *other* than the outside limit
of being Human we all share: they week no career in Film, nor
Video either, but rather earn their worldly living otherwise, save
money enough for rolls of film, one at a time (potential jewel/
each frame), expose the silver halides to their, each his/her, electrical innards as much as to the bounce-light of the phenomenological world, then edit as true to each his or her particularities
of memory as is emotionally possible, in touch with that buzz
of The Mind known as Muse.

These, mostly unknown filmmakers, work with the medium
in absolutely traditional ways, those ways we naturally associate
with composers, poets, painters (some painting directly on film),
all alone, or with help of a few friends, often projecting their
camera-originals (unable to afford a print), living lives close to
the ground, the bone, "poor folk, but happy," as I know them,
now, in the living rooms of their projection, in pursuit of something as ephemeral as unanswerable Mystery...out of a dedica-
tion to something as ineffably intimate as Aesthetic Form — this
activity of the artist the human norm-in-Time which eventually,
inexorably but gently, informs us all.

[May 26, 1992]

Dog Stur Man

inspirations

When I, and most of my contemporaries, were making films as 'kin to poetry as we could imagine, THEN the European avant-garde was, indeed, of some considerable influence upon American filmmaking. The Museum of Modern Art in New York City regularly showed *The Andalusian Dog* of Bunuel/Dali, Cocteau's *Blood of a Poet*, *Entre'Acte* by Rene Clair, and some several Man Ray films, including the Ray/Duchamp collaboration of annotated whirling discs, *Anemic Cinema*.

Primarily, though, the 1940s and 1950s European movie fare consisted of Italian Neo-Realism, Russian "classic" cinema, Dreyer and Cocteau: the "feature" films of these narrative-dramatic makers came to local "art cinema" venues throughout the United States. I, for instance, first realized (senior year of high school in Denver, Colorado) that "the movies" MIGHT/ (possibly) be an Art Form, during my third or fourth viewing of Cocteau's *Orpheus*, followed similarly that summer of 1949 by sub-titled screenings of *Beauty and the Beast* of Cocteau, then DiSica and Rossallini features, Dreyer's *Day of Wrath*, in several Denver neighborhood movie houses. Shortly thereafter I rediscovered Orson Welles, his *Macbeth* and sometime later *Othello* (though one must realize that the then-controversial *Citizen Kane* was not available to audiences in the U.S. until the '60s).

Many American filmmakers who inspired my work (Watson /Webber, Kenneth Anger, James Broughton & Sidney Peter-son, Gregory Markopoulos, Mass & Menken, and Joseph Cornell, for a few examples) were obviously inspired by the European avant-garde; but I must confess that (excepting only Eisenstein and Cocteau) I was not, in my youth, particularly affected by cinema's "Europeans"—only, rather, INdirectly affected through my U.S. contemporaries...and, of that, only finally deeply by N.Y.C.'s Marie Menken and Joseph Cornell. This is perhaps because I, early on, developed an aversion to Surrealism—finding it an altogether inadequate (highly symbolic) envisionment of dreaming.[1]

What DID rivet my attention (and must be particularly distinguished) was Jean-Isadore Isou's *Venom and Eternity*: as a creative polemic it has no peer in the history of cinema (several years ago I was greatly moved to see some of Maurice Lemaitre's work, and I was delighted to know that this man, who began work with Isou, had continued in this, by now his own, rich vein of making).

I must also confess that because of my deep-rooted sense of the dream inadequacies of Surrealism, I was never inspired in my work by Joseph Cornell's boxes or collages—only, essentially, by his completely distinctive films (two of which I helped him to make): but Marie Menken did seem, and does seem, to me to be (despite her limited output) a kind of "Gertrude Stein of filmmaking"' and Menken's films (except when she's collaborating with Dwight Ripley or her husband Willard Maas) have almost *no* relationship to European aesthetics. Menken's work is, as I take my own to be, best epitomized by reference to "No ideas but in things," as conceived and practiced in language by the American poet William Carlos Williams—by his whole, and very celebrated poem "The Red Wheel-barrow," *so forth!*

On these, my, non-Surreal "grounds," it is the stuff of the world, material—nay, matter itself—which one would aesthetically separate oneself from and directly incorporate, or parallel, in the making of any such "paradigm" we might come to recognize as "Art." I do NOT mean that one, certainly not THIS one, would "hold a mirror up to Nature" (as Milton suggested was the habit of Shakespeare), etcetera, NOR one would "incorporate" in the sense that the european collage artists, or Cornell, included material objects in their various arts (and as I did in making my film *Mothlight* out of moth-wings, flowers, leaves); but rather that the/any maker of aesthetic aspiration would have no ideas but in things.

But here's "the rub" appropo that, for a would-be "artist" filmmaker: all photographed imagery is quite obviously, thus adamantly, REpresentational—i.e. that the/any photographed film tends always to exist referentially AND in an implied past tense...always therefore tied to a remembrance, or resemblance of "Things Past," an ideology of Memory, the ideas of Memorial. Much of my life's work constitutes an attempt to subvert the representation photography IS by creating a sense of constant present-tense in each film's every instant of viewing — that, for one example, all nameable, thus referential, images in a film be referential within the film. This I think, is intrinsically American...which might bring us, as it does me in most of my making, to Gertrude Stein again...her literary triumph of the full presence of consciousness, present tense...(or such as U.S. poet Charles Olson's "There is no history except as it is invoked in The Present" (to paraphrase from conversation)).

It could also bring us to consideration of Marie Menken again: her hand-held camera directly capturing external light shaped into representational images on film) is, at the same time, recording her whole body's reaction to what she is seeing through that camera. She always tended, when taking pictures, to DANCE and, when editing those film strips, then, to capture the eye's dance (rather than, say, some idealized stance-dance of "the mind's eye"). She would hang up the strips of film and study the patterns, right, left, up, down, and splice them together as designs in Time—plenty of ideas arising in these arrangements of rhythmic Form, but no superimposed ideology.[2]

Menken's films generate exquisite maxims of the physiology which made them (in conjunction with the physical objects which originally excited her to photograph them and the space through which she'd moved to accomplish that in accordance with her timing...the tempo and rhythm of her being, in this perceptive act, emotionally moved). These recognitions, in my youth, prompted by the "hands on"/hand-painted and etched works of such makers as Isou (and Lemaitre as recently seen), Len Lye, Harry Smith, Carolee Schneemann, along with the printed works of George Méliès, Fernand Zecca, Wallace Berman, Robert Breer, Kenneth Anger, Bruce Conner, Diana Barrie, Hollis Frampton, Victor Facinto, Emily Breer, Eric Waldmar, John Writer, Carl Fuerman, Katherine Kenworth, Fred Worden, Caroline Avery, Phil Solomon, Cecile Fontaine, Donna Cameron, Karen Albano, The Silt Group, Luther Price, Mark Street, Jennifer Reeves, Arianne Gerstein, and especially (the last several years) Peter Herwitz, as well as **ANON** known and unknown to me, have all directly inspired me in my current filmmaking.

I now no longer photograph, but rather paint upon clear strips of film—essentially freeing myself from the dilemmas of re-presentation. I aspire to a visual music, a "music" for the eyes (as my films are entirely without sound-tracks these days). Just as a composer can be said to work primarily with "musical ideas," I can be said to work with the ideas intrinsic to film, which is the only medium capable of making paradigmatic "closure" apropos Primal Sight. A composer most usually creates parallel to the soundings of the inner ear—the primary thought of sounds; I, similarly, now work with the electric synapses of thought to achieve overall cathexis paradigms separate from but "at one" with the inner lights, The Light at source, of being human.

[June 8, 1996]

1.It should be noted that, although Jean Cocteau (my initial filmic mentor) WAS a card-carrying Surrealist, he was always the "bad boy" of that movement, always moving against-the-grain of Surrealist aesthetics, and was eventually "ex-communicated" from Surrealism by Andre Breton himself.

2. There is one film by Menken, *Hurry! Hurry!*, which does utilize superimposition to express an idealistic notion (that sperm exists in a knd of hell): she superimposed microscopically photographed spermatazoa with flames; but by the time she has rhythmically coordinated every minute move of the sperm with each fractional second's flicker of flame, a metaphysical experiencing of the film overrides her original thought and engenders an otherwise ineffable meditation on fire and physiology.

selected film annotations

Aftermath *(1981)*
The raw meat of the mind's imagination, the pounding blood of it, attempting to erase (rather than assimilate) a televised movie of ferocious popular appeal...a life versus death struggle played out in the purely visual (anti-numerical) area of thought. 16mm, 8 min., color, silent.

@ *(1979)*
The first film of mine which is so very much there where it's at THAT it deserves visual symbol as title and no further explanation from me at/et? all. 16mm, 6 min., color, silent.

Angels' *(1971)*
This then the property of many angels. 16mm, 2 min., color, silent.

Anticipation of the Night *(1958)*
The daylight shadow of a man in its movement evokes lights in the night. A rose bowl held in hand reflects both sun and moon like illumination. The opening of a doorway onto trees anticipates the twilight into the night. A child is born on the lawn, born of water with its promissory rainbow, and the wild rose. It becomes the moon and the source of all light. Lights of the night become young children playing a circular game. The moon moves over a pillared temple to which all lights return. There is seen the sleep of innocents in their animal dreams, becoming the amusement, their circular game, becoming the morning. The trees change color and lose their leaves for the morn, they become the complexity of branches in which the shadow man hangs himself. 16mm, 42 min., color, silent.

Aquarien *(1974)*
"EN"?—as the dictionary has it: "made of, of or belonging to" (as I have it) Aquarious/an(d) so forth: Latin water carrier in the sky, etc. This is my first fully conscious "tone poem" film. 16mm, 5 min., color, silent.

Arabic Numeral Series *(1980-81)*
This series of [19] films, each extraordinarily unique from every other (except "0 + 10" going together) is inspired and governed by strata of the mind's moving-visual-thinking different from that of the *Roman Numeral Series*...or perhaps one should say that the Arabic Numerals come to fruition thru some tree-of-nerves separate from that which gave birth to the *Romans* (as it is physiologically deceptive to think of thought in "layers"). The Arabics range in length from approximately five minutes to 32 minutes and may be projected at 24fps as well as 18, tho' the latter speed seems preferable for starts. I think each film's integrity of rhythm would allow viewing at a greater variety of

speeds, were there the 16mm projectors to permit that exercise. So far as I can tell, they defy verbal interpretation (even more than their Roman equivalents) and would, thus, seem to be closer to Music than any previous work given me to do; but if that be true, it is (as composer James Tenney put it to me) that they relate to that relatively small area of musical composition which resists Song and Dance and exists more purely in terms of Sound Events in Time/ Space. Finally, then, the inspiration of all those modern (and a few ancient) composers I've most loved since my teens overwhelms the easier, and comfortably lovely, habits of jig and do-re-mi AND creates a visual correlative OF music's eventuality—i.e., each *Arabic* is formed by the intrinsic grammar of the most inner (perhaps pre-natal) structure of thought itself. 16mm, color, silent

The Art of Vision *(1961-1965)*
Includes the complete *Dog Star Man* and is a full extension of the singular visible themes of it. Inspired by that period of music in which the word *symphonia* was created and by the thought that the term, as then, was created to name the overlap and enmeshing of suites, this film presents the visual symphony that *Dog Star Man can be seen as* and also all the suites of which it is composed. But as it is a film, not work of music, the above suggests only *one* of the possible approaches to it. For instance as "cinematographer," at source, means "writer of movement," certain poetic analogies might serve as well. The form is conditioned by the works of arts which have inspired *Dog Star Man,* its growth of form by the physiology and experiences (including experiences of art) of the man who made it. Finally it must be seen for what it is. 16mm, 270 min., color, silent.

Babylon Series *(1989)*
After a six or seven year study of Hammurabi's Code, original Babylonian text and translation, I've tried to feel my way into the moving visual thought process of this ancient culture (whose numerical system is composed primarily of building materials, nails, joints and the like): this, then, is a visual music which balances the two thought processes of Structure and Nature. 16mm, 6 min, color, silent.

Babylon Series #2 *(1990)*
Out of the vagueries of sometime beseeming repetitive light patterns, and the delicately variable rhythms of thought process, the imagination of The Monumental and of the Ephemeral are born to mind hard as nails. 16mm, 5 min., color, silent.

Babylon Series #3 *(1990)*
There is an architectured garden of the variably brash rock-solid liquid-encompassing, but always imitative, human mind as it processes the given light thoughtfully. This film is about that. 16mm, 6 min., color, silent.

Bird *(1978)*
This the first clear vision I've had of the hot-blooded dinosaurs still living among us. 16mm, 4 min., color, silent.

Black Vision *(1965)*
...is inspired by the only passage in Jean Paul Sartre's writings which has ever specifically concerned me—the passage from *Nausea* wherein the protagonist sits in a park and imagines his suicide. 16mm, 3 min., b/w, silent.

Burial Path *(1978)*
The film begins with the image of a dead bird. The mind moves to forget, as well as to remember: this film, in the tradition of *Thot-Fal'n,* graphs the process of forgetfulness against all oddities of remembered bird-shape. The film might best be seen along with *Sirius Remembered* and *The Dead* as the third part of a trilogy. In Memoriam: Donald Sutherland. 16mm, 8 min., color, silent.

The Cat of the Worm's Green Realm *(1997)*
Flares of color break into streams of light, leaves, wood grain and prism-etched vegetation. / A moon lifts out of this dark weave to be replaced by autumn leaves against a grainy sky, a fiery sky. / The moon, again, caught in clouds. The movements, moonlit, of a cat. Vegetation and toned flares (a kind of "ghost light" midst microscopic photography of leaves and twigs). / A gray cat licks itself, its name-tag reflected in lens refractions midst microscopic visions of ice and snow, autumn leaves, green leaves, a distant snow-laden green scene. / A black cat sits quickly down on a green lawn. A night of shards of forms in darkness passes into a day again...again an octagonal light shape "echoing" the cat's name-tag midst, now, colored leaves in extreme close-up and at some distance mixed with sun. Again a "night" of showering dark, a "dawn" of pinks and yellows of plant growth in close-up. / A kind of gentle yellow "high noon" prevails into which the orange worm appears and reappears, twisting, arching, turning. A phosphorescent orange of leaves explodes midst greens and black holes appropriate to the image of the worm. / Flares of suns, imprismd midst yellows and greens and vibrant sky blues ...always the forms of many varieties of leafage mix with a veritable rain or clash of oveerall tones, a fire of forms, a glowing color photo-negative of worm, and the final canopies of autumn tone and sky tone permeated by sun, sun streaks and octagonal prism shapes *ad infinitum.* 16mm, 18 min., color, silent.

Centre *(1978)*
A series of narrative events, stories if you like, but so clustered visually as to have a center, so to speak, slightly off centre. 16mm, 10 min., color, silent.

Chartres Series *(1994)*
A year and a half ago the filmmaker Nick Dorsky, hearing I was going to France, insisted I must see the Chartres Cathedral. I, who had studied picture

books of its great stained-glass windows, sculpture and architecture for years, having also read Henry Adams' great book three times, willingly complied and had an experience of several hours (in the discreet company of French filmmaker Jean-Michele Bouhours) which surely transformed my aesthetics more than any other single experience. Then Marilyn's sister died; and I, who could not attend the funeral, sat down alone and began painting on film one day, this death in mind…Chartres in mind. Eight months later the painting was completed on four little films which comprise a suite in homage to Chartres and dedicated to Wendy Jull. 16mm, 9 min., color, silent.

A Child's Garden and the Serious Sea *(1991)*
In poet Ronald Johnson's great epic, Ark, in the first book *Foundations*, the poem "Beam 29" has this passage: "The seed is disseminated at the gated mosaic a hundred feet / below, above / long windrows of motion / connecting dilated arches undergoing transamplifications: / 'seen in the water so clear as christiall' / (prairie tremblante)" which breaaks into musical notation that, "presto," becomes a design of spatial tilts: This is where the film began; and I carried a xerox of the still unpublished ARC 50 through 66 all that trip with Marilyn and Anton around Vancouver Island. As I wrote him, "The pun 'out on a limn' kept ringing through my mind as I caught the hairs of side-light off ephemera of objects tangent to Marilyn's childhood: She grew up in Victoria; and there I was in her childhood backyard…": and then there was The Sea— not as counter-balance but as hidden generator of it all, of The World to be discovered by the/any child…as poet Charles Olson has it: "Vast earth rejoices, / deep-swirling Okeanos steers all things through all things, / everything issues from the one, the soul is led from drunkenness / to dryness, the sleeper lights up from the dead, / the man awake lights up from the sleeping" (*Maximus*, from "Dogtown–I"). 16mm, 80 min, color, silent.

Christ Mass Sex Dance *(1991)*
This word, composed of six rolls of superimposed images set to Jim Tenney's electronic music track "Blue Suede," is a celebration of the balletic restraints of adolescent sexuality-shaped (in this instance) by "The Nutcracker Suite" of Tchaikovsky as well as the gristly roots of Elvis Presley. 16mm, 5.5 min, color, sound.

Clancy *(1974)*
This is a portrait of the man I choose to call "the greatest I've known": Clancy, whom the fates surnamed Sheehy, personifies for me that which is simply human beyond condition and all conditioning. 16mm, 4.5 min., color, silent.

Commingled Containers *(1997)*
This "return to photography" (after several years of only painting film) was made on the eve of cancer surgery—a kind of "last testament," if you will…an envisionment of the fleeting complexity of worldly phenomenon. 16mm, 5 min., color, silent.

Confession *(1986)*

This film was photographed midst the drama it depicts: As I was the "protagonist" of the drama, it is the most extremely autobiographical documentation given to me to do. As it was made while the brain was thus stunned, I think it was wrongly titled *Love Sacrifice*. I am now renaming it *Confession* (in the same spirit which moved me to retitle *Sincerity IV / Duplicity I*. There is a clear sense that all which the film depicts precludes even the possibilities of Love, so that it represents an even greater sacrifice of all that we know of loving than I had originally thought when I first titled it. Perhaps I, after all a filmmaker, should cease speaking and simply turn to a quoate from Petrarch which seems true "addenda" to the film now, as it did when I made it: "Firstly, I revealed in salutary confession the secret filth of my misdeeds, which had long been festering in stagnant silence; and I made it my custom to confess often, and thus to display the wounds of my blinded soul to the almighty Healer" (*Epistolae Familiares X*, 5, June 11, probably 1352). I suddenly thought the title might best be, simply *Confession*; for the Petrarch does hold solid thru all this turmoil. I continue to think there can be no "wrong" form of loving...BUT, people can become easily confused as to what Love IS. 16mm, 24 min., color, silent.

The Dead *(1960)*

Europe weighted down so much with that past, was *The Dead*. I was always Tourist there; I couldn't live in it. The graveyard could stand for all my view of Europe, for all the concerns with past art, for involvement with symbol. *The Dead* became my first work in which things that might very easily be taken as symbols were so photographed as to destroy all their symbolic potential. The action of making *The Dead* kept me alive. 16mm, 11 min., color, silent.

Deus Ex *(1971)*

I have been many times very ill in hospitals; and I drew on all that experience while making *Deus Ex* in West Penn. Hospital of Pittsburgh: but I was especially inspired by the memory of one incident in an Emergency Room of S.F.'s Mission District: while waiting for medical help, I had held myself together by reading an April-May, 1965 issue of *Poetry Magazine;* and the following lines from Charles Olson's "Cole's Island" had especially centered the experience, "touchstone" of *Deus Ex,* for me: Charles begins the poem with the statement, "I met Death—" and then: "He didn't bother me, or say anything. Which is/ not surprising, a person might not, in the circumstances;/ or at most a nod or something. Or they would. But they wouldn't,/ or you wouldn't think to either, if it was Death. And/ He certainly was, the moment I saw him." The film begins with this sense of such an experience and goes on to envision the whole battle of hospital on these grounds, thru the heart surgery seen as equivalent to Aztec ritual sacrifice...the lengths men go to avoid so simple and straight a relationship with Death as Charles Olson managed on/ in "Cole's Island." 16mm, 35 min., color, silent.

Door *(1971)*
This is the only all-inclusive autobiography I've yet managed; and as I'm still alive, it is to be understood as a metaphor which defines the limits of expectation. 16mm, 2 min., color, silent.

Duplicity *(1978)*
A friend of many years' acquaintance showed me the duplicity of myself. And, midst guilt and anxiety, I came to see that duplicity often shows itself forth in semblance of sincerity. Then a dream informed me that *Sincerity IV,* which I had just completed, was such a semblance. The dream ended with the word "Duplicity" scratched white across the closed eyelid (as the title *The Weir-Falcon Saga* had been given to me). I saw that the film in question demonstrated a duplicity of relationship between the Brakhages and animals (Totemism) and environs (especially trees), visiting friends (Robert Creeley, Ed Dorn, Donald Sutherland, Angelo DiBenedetto and Jerome Hill among them) and people-at-large. I saw that the film shifted its compositions equally along a line of dark shapes as well as light, and that it did not progress (as did earlier Sincerities) but was rather a correlative of *Sincerity III.* Accordingly I changed the title to *Duplicity.* 16mm, 23 min., color, silent.

Duplicity II *(1978)*
This, the second film of the continuing autobiographical Duplicity series, is composed of superimpositions much as the mind 'dupes' remembered experience into some semblance of, say, composed surety rather than imbalanced accuracy—as thought may even warp 'scene into symmetry, or 'face' into multitudinous mask. What will have been becomes what will *be being.* I've tried to 'give the lie' to this genesis of all white-lying. 16mm, 20 min., color, silent.

Duplicity III *(1980)*
The final Duplicity in this series does seem a resolve with the term. All previous visual manifestations have been extended (thru 4-roll superimpositions) to their limit. Obvious costumes and masks, Drama as an ultimate play- for-truth, and totemic recognition of human *animal* life-on-earth dominate all the evasions duplicity otherwise affords. 16mm, 30 min. (18fps), color, silent.

Eye Myth *(1972, 1981)*
190 frames, begun in 1968 as sketch for *The Horseman, The Woman, and The Moth.*

eyes *(1971)*
After wishing for years to be given-the-opportunity of filming some of the more "mystical" occupations of our Times—some of the more obscure Public Figures which the average imagination turns into "bogeymen"...viz.: Policemen, Doctors, Soldiers, Politicians, etc.: —I was at last permitted to ride in a Pittsburgh Policecar, camera in hand, the final several days of Sept. 1970— this opportunity largely due to the efforts of a Pittsburgh newspaper photog-

rapher, Mike Chikiris…who was sympathetic to my film show at The Carnegie Institute and responded to my wish as stated on that occasion—therefore pleaded my "cause" eloquently with Police Inspectors of his acquaintance: my thanks to him, to Sally Dixon of The Carnegie Institute and to the Policemen who created the situation that made this film possible. / As to the film itself: "Polis is eyes," said Charles Olson, having found the archeological root of the word-end (thus beginning) of, say, "metropolis," etc. 'Police is a clear etymological derivative of 'polis'." / The more currently popular fix on these terms comes from, say, Dashiel Hammet's "private eye," & the sense of response-ability which Raymond Chandler and even Ross MacDonald give to their detective heros under that term. / The Police, then, are the public eyes; and they are, thus, expected to be Specialists of that ability-to respond which most of the rest of the society has lost all Metro sense-of. / The experience of making this film prompted that clarity of terms: "Polis is eyes" was my constant prayer, to make that experience clear, the last entire day of photographing. / The film mostly assembled, rather than edited, is thus the surest track I could make of what it was given to me to see. / It is "framed" by clouds and the ocean for the simplest reasons of "perspective." 16mm, 35 min., color, silent.

Fifteen Song Traits *(1965, 1980)*

A series of individual portraits of friends and family, all inter-related in what might be called a branch growng directly from the trunk of *Songs 1* thru *14.* In order of appearance: Robert Kelly, Jane and our dog Dunn, our boys Bearthm and Rarc, daughter Crystal and the canary Cheep Donkey, Robert Creeley and Michael McClure, the rest of our girls Myrrena and Neowyn, Angelo DiBenedetto, Ed Dorn and his family, and Jonas Mekas (to whom the whole of the *Fifteen Song Traits* is dedicated), as well as some few strangers, were the source of these *Traits* coming into being—my thanks to all…and to all who see them clearly. 16mm, 31 min., color, silent.

Films By Stan Brakhage *(1961)*

I had a camera with which I could make multiple superimpositions spontaneously. It had been lent to me for a week. I was also given a couple of rolls of color film which had been through an intensive fire. The chance that the film would not record any image at all left me free to experiment and to try to create the sense of the daily world in which we live, and what it meant to me. I wanted to record our home, and yet deal with it as being that area from which the films by Stan Brakhage arise, and to try to make one arise at the same time…. 16mm, 4.5 min., color, silent.

Fire of Waters *(1965)*

Inspired by a statement in a letter from poet Robert Kelly: "The truth of the matter is this that: man lives in a fire of waters and will live eternally in the first taste"—this film is a play of light and sounds upon that theme. 16mm, 7 min., b/w, sound.

Flight *(1974)*

Pun on "light" intended—that short preceeding expellation of breath perhaps the "subject matter" of this film which centers in consideration of death. It is the third tone poem film and did much surprise me by thus completing a trilogy of the "4 classical Elements."16mm, 5.5 min., color, silent.

Fox Fire Child Watch *(1971)*

Ken, Flo, and Nisi Jacobs in the Syracuse Airport: this is what you might call baby-sitting in the swamp. 16mm, 3 min., color, silent.

The God of Day Had Gone Down Upon Him *(2000)*

This film of single-strand photography begins with the "fire" of reflective light on water and on the barest inferences of a ship. Throughout, the interwoven play of light and water tell the inferred "tale" of the film through rhythm, the tempo, through visible textures and forms in gadual evolution, through resultant "moods" generated by these modes of making, and, then, by the increasingly distant boat images, birds, animals, fleeting silhouettes of people and their artifacts, flotsam and jetsam of the sea-dead, as well as (near end, and almost as at a funeral) flowers in bloom, swallowed by darkness midst the crumbling of the sand castles. These nameable objects (sometimes, at first, quite enigmatic) are the frets of Symbol; but always the symbolic content is swept back into the weave of sea and light and seen, as is the merry-go-round near the beginning of the film, or the horizontally photographed fountain mimicking incoming ocean waves, to be as if spawned in the mind during oceanic contemplation. In fact, the structure of the entire film might be characterized thus: meditation on ocean is interrupted continually by rapidly cut visual frets of (at first) irritated thought; but then gradually across the course of the film these fraughts of symbols and rapidly edited constructs become a calm 'kin to resignation, become more at-one with the diminishing light and incoming waves. The turning point of the film is near its midpoint where tall and relatively violent waves smash their cold and fearsome colors left to right across the screen, interwoven with an old man sitting in a dark blue room, followed by hints of backyard fences, grasses, distant ephemeral flowers and a hung whirling decoration. Reminders of this midpoint are accomplished through visual rhymes such as similarities of blue and a madly whirling kite against a bright sky, as well as by the (near end) entire sequence in which multiple garish flowers invade the (by then) almost fully meditative sea imagery. There are visual rhymes also connecting this work with its two previous "parts" *(A Child's Garden and the Serious Sea* and *The Mammals of Victoria),* such as an orange ball attached to a boat which "rhymes" with thrown orange balls in the previous film. As the whole film is stitched with red-orange-yellow flares (indicators of light-struck sections at beginning and ending of individual 100-foot rolls (making of the film a distinctive sequential evolution), so the end of the film has a slight flare-up (or fillip of hope?) after burgeoning dark. 16mm, 50 min., color, silent.

The Governor *(1977)*

On July 4th, 1976, I and my camera toured the state of Colorado with Governor Richard D. Lamm, as he traveled in parades with his children, appeared at dinners, lectured, etc. On July 20th, I spent the morning in his office in the state capitol and the afternoon with himself and his wife in a television studio, then with Mrs. Lamm greeting guests to the governor's mansion and finally with Governor Lamm in his office again. These two days of photography took me exactly one year to edit into a film which wove itself thru multiple superimpositions into a study of light and power. 16mm, 58 min, color, silent.

"he was born, he suffered, he died" *(1974)*

The quote is Joseph Conrad answering a critic who found his books too long. Conrad replied that he could write a novel on the inside of a matchbook cover, thus (as above), but that he "preferred to elaborate." The "Life" of the film is scratched on black leader. The "elaboration" of color tonalities is as the mind's eye responds to hieroglyph. 16mm, 8 min., color, silent.

The Horseman, The Woman, and The Moth *(1968)*

A long myth drawn directly onto the film's surface, which is painted, dyed, treated so that it will grow controlled crystals and mold—as textures of the figures and forms of the drama—, some images stamped thru melted wax crayon techniques, some images actual objects (such as moth wings) collaged directly on the celluloid...so that the protagonists of this myth (as listed in the title) weave thru crystalline structures and organic jungles of the colorful world of hypnogogic vision—edited into "themes and variations" that tell "a thousand and one" stories while, at the same time, evoking Baroque music...the primary musical inspiration being the harpsichord sonatas of Domenico Scarlatti. 16mm, 19.5 min, color, silent.

In Consideration of Pompeii *(1995)*

Since the age of 17/18, I've been haunted by the catastrophe of Pompeii—beginning with photographs (sold as pornography in high school) of the mummified lovers caught in coitus and preserved by the volcanic ash, revivified by many ghostly photographic books, but especially illuminated by Donald Sutherland's accounts and images from first hand experience of the ruins. Finally my homage in three parts: "The Flowers of Pompeii," "Ashen Snow," and "Angelus." 16mm, 5 min., color, silent.

The Loom *(1986)*

Dedicated to Robert Kelly. A multiple-superimposition hand-painted visual symphony of animal life of earth. *The Loom* might be compared to musical-quartet form (as there are almost always four superimposed pictures); but the complexity of texture, multiplicity of tone, and the variety of interrelated rhythm, suggest symphonic dimensions. The film is very inspired by George Méliès: the animals exist (in Jane's enclosure) as on a stage, their inter-relationships edited to the disciplines of dance, so therefore one might say this hardly represents "animal life on earth"; but I would argue that this work at least epitomizes theatrical Nature, magical Creature, and is the outside limit, to date, of my art in that respect. (The balance-of-light was so perfectly realized in making the neg. of this print that I wish to credit Western Cine Lab's "timer" Louise Fujiki as creative collaborator in the accomplishment of this work.) 16mm, 43.5 min., color, silent.

Lovemaking *(1966)*
An American Kama Sutra—Love's answer to filmic pornography...four visions of sexual loving which exist in an aesthetic balance of feeling the very opposite of the strip-tease as usually encountered in both Hollywood movies and the foreign, so-called "Art Film": a totally new experience. 16mm, 36 min., color, silent.

Made Manifest *(1980)*
"Every man's work shall be made manifest, for the day shall declare it, because it shall be revealed by fire and the fire shall try every man's work of what sort it is."—*I Corinthians 111-113*. 16mm, 12 min., color, silent.

The Mammals of Victoria *(1994)*
The film begins with a series of horizontally running ocean tide waves, sometimes with mountains in the background, hand-painted patterns, sometimes step-printed hand-painting, abstractions composed of distorted (jammed) TV shapes in shades of blue with occasional red, refractions of light within the camera lens, sometimes mixed with reflections of water— this "weave" of imagery occasionally revealing recognizable shapes of birds and humans, humans as fleeting figures in the water, as distant shapes in a rowboat, as human shadows, so forth. Increasingly closer images of water, and of light reflected off water, as well as of bursts of fire, intersperse the long shots, the seascapes and all the other interwoven imagery. Eventually a distant volleyball arcs across the sky filled with cumulus clouds: this is closely followed by, and interspersed with, silhouettes of a young man and woman in the sea, which leads to some extremely out-of-focus images from a front car window, an opening between soft-focus trees, a clearing. Carved wooden teeth suddenly sweep across the frame. Then the film ends on some soft-focus horizon lines, foregrounded by ocean, slowly rising and falling and rising again in the frame. This film is a companion piece to *A Child's Garden and The Serious Sea*. 16mm, 30 min., color, silent.

Mothlight *(1963)*
What a moth might see from birth to death if black were white and white were black. 16mm, 4 min., color, silent.

Murder Psalm *(1981)*
"...unparalleled debauchery, when man turns into a filthy, cowardly, cruel,

vicious reptile. That's what we need! And what's more, a little 'fresh blood' that we may grow accustomed to it…(Dostoyevsky, *The Devils*, Part II, Chapter VIII). "In my novel *The Devils* I attempted to depict the complex and heterogeneous motives which may prompt even the purest of heart and the most naive people to take part in an absolutely monstrous crime" (Dostoyevsky, *The Diary of a Writer*). 16mm, 18.5 min., color, silent.

Nightmare Series *(1978)*
Four films so related to each other as to be an equivalent of that frightful dreaming which makes Wake of the following day, so that it be spent mourning the events of the night. A decade and a half ago, poet Robert Kelly told me that the "crucial work" of our Time might be what he calls "the dream work": I hope, with this *Series,* to have entertained his challenge more thoughtfully than with any previous "dream" filmmaking. In homage to Sigmund Freud and Surrealism, this film proposes clear visible alternatives to the consideration of both "The Interpretation of…" and all previous representation of…dreaming. 16mm, 20.5 min, color, silent.

Pasht *(1965)*
In honor of the cat, so named, and the goddess of all cats which she was named after (that taking shape in the Egyptian mind of the spirit of cats), and of birth (as she was then giving kittens when the pictures were taken), of sex as source, and finally of death (as this making was the salvage therefrom and in memoriam). 16mm, 6.5 min., color, silent.

The Presence *(1972)*
The Presence reflects some sight of Insect as Being. The imagined aura and environment of a beetle creates a "world" wherein this solitary insect may simply be seen. 16mm, 3.5 min., color, silent.

The Process *(1972)*
LIGHT was primary in my consideration. All senses of "process" are (to me) based primarily on "thought-process"; and "thought-process" is based primarily on "memory re-call"; and that, as any memory process (all process finally) is electrical (firing of nerve connection) and expresses itself most clearly as a "back-firing" of nerve endings in the eye which DO become visible to us (usually eyes closed) as "brain movies"—as Michael McClure calls them. When we are not re-constructing "a scene" (recalling something once seen), then we are watching (on the "screen" of closed eye-lids) the very PROCESS itself…. 16mm, 8 min., color, silent.

Purity And After *(1978)*
Two short films, the first NOT about purity itself, whatever that might be, but rather an equivalent of the process of searching for purity in the mind… the second film, then, thought's rebound from that. 16mm, 5.5 min., color, silent.

The Riddle of Lumen *(1972)*

The classical riddle was meant to be heard, of course. Its answers are contained within its questions; and on the smallest piece of itself this possibility depends: upon SOUND—"utterly," like they say...the pun its pivot. Therefore, my *Riddle of Lumen* depends upon qualities of LIGHT. All films do, of course. But with *The Riddle Of Lumen,* "the hero" of the film is light/itself. It is a film I'd long wanted to make—inspired by the sense, and specific formal possibilities, of the classical Eng.-lang. riddle...only one appropriate to film and, thus, as distinct from language as I could make it. 16mm, 14.5 min., color, silent.

Roman Numeral Series *(1979-1980)*

The Roman Numeral Series is dedicated to Don Yannacito. 16mm, 2.5 to 10.5 min. each, color, silent.

I This begins a new series of films which would ordinarily be called "abstract," "non-objective," "non-representational," etc. I cannot tolerate any of those terms and, in fact, had to struggle against all such historical concepts to proceed with my work. Midst creative process, the sound "imagnostic" kept ringing in my ears. It seems to be an enjambment of Latin and Greek; but Charlton T. Lewis' "Elementary Latin Dictionary" gives me (via Guy Davenport) "image"...Sanscrit = AIC = "like," GNOSIS "knowledge," GNOSTIC AGNOSCO = "to recognize"/ "to know" and the happier IMAGINOSUS "full of fancies"/"fantasies," illustrated by Catullus' singular use (perhaps creation of the term?) in the line "His mind solidly filled with fancies of a girl." Even though exhausted by this etymological pursuit, and despite my prejudice against taking on "foreign airs" of tongue, "Imagnostic," keeps singing in my head and escaping my lips in conversation. I'm not sure if this work is titled "I" for "Imagnostic," or "I" as designating first person singular, or "I" Roman Numeral One.

II Now that *II* has been completed, one would suppose that the above film *I* is "One"...unless, of course, this film's spoken title is "aye-aye" or even, perhaps, slyly referring to the two "eyes" which made it, as distinct from the singularity of vision which flattens space in the making of its predecessor.

III The third in this series of Imagnostic Films seems particularly magic to me inasmuch as I cannot even remember the photographic source of these images or, thus, of having taken them.

IV It was while studying this film that I decided to group these "romans" under the title *Roman Numeral Series* and to give up the term "imagnostic" altogether...also to dedicate the series to Don Yannacito who had seen something "concrete" and even narratively dramatic in this work. The term "deja vu" comes to mind each time I view this film—this, then, somehow the "echoing" of the birth of imagery.

V An imagery sharp as stars and hard as the thought-universe (turning back upon itself) absorbed in gentle patterns ofcontemplation.

VI What shall one say?

VII What CAN one say?—that won't limit, by language, the complexity of mov-

ing visual thinking?...the skein of pattern that seeks to make its own language.
VIII   This the most formal of all these works.
IX   This the most absolute.

Salome *(1980)*

Portrait of the great chess master, aesthetician, human being Eugene Salome.
16mm, 3.5 min., color, silent.

Scenes From Under Childhood: Sections 1-4 *(1967-1970)*

A visualization of the inner world of foetal beginnings, the infant, the baby,
the child—a shattering of the "myths of childhood" through revelation of
the extremes of violent terror and overwhelming joy of that world darkened
to most adults by their sentimental remembering of it...a "tone poem" for
the eye—very inspired by the music of Olivier Messiaen. 16mm, 135 min.,
color, silent.

Sexual Meditation No. 1: Motel *(1970,1980)*

This film was originally photographed in 1970 in regular 8mm. It has now (a
decade later) been blown-up to 16mm so that it can join the rest of the Sexual
Meditation Series. 8mm, 6 min, color, silent.

Sexual Meditation: Room with View *(1971)*

Directly in the tradition of *Sexual Meditiation No.1: Motel* (first available *only* in
8mm), this "sequel" does explore further the possibilities of nudes in a room.
16mm, 4 min., color, silent.

Sexual Meditation: Open Field *(1973)*

This film takes all the masturbatory themes of previous Sexual Mediations
back to source in pre-adolescent dreams. *Open Field* is in the mind, of course,
and exists as a weave of trees, grasses, waters and bodies poised and fleeting
at childhood's end. The scene is lit as by sun and moon alike and haunted by
the pursuant adult. 16mm, 6.5 min., color, silent.

The Shores of Phos: A Fable *(1972)*

Phos = Light, but then I did also want that word within the title which would
designate *place,* as within the nationalities of "the fabulous"—a specific country of the imagination with tangible shores, etc. The film adheres strictly to
the ordinary Form of the classical fable. 16mm, 10.5 min., color, silent.

Short Films 1975: 1-10

This is a series of ten deliberately untitled films, each separated on the reel by
several feet of black leader. 16mm, 38 min., color, silent.

Short Films: 1976

Four films verging on portraiture, converging to make a drama for all seasons,
starring: Jane Brakhage as The Dreamer; Bob Benson as the Magnificent

Stranger; Omar Beagle as The Snow Plow Man; Jimmy Ryan Morris as The Poet, and as Doc Holliday. 16mm, 21 min., color, silent.

Sincerity *(1973)*

This, the first completed reel of work-in-progress, draws on autobiographical energies and images which reflect the first 20 years of my living. I have three definitions of the word "sincerity" to sustain my working along these lines of thought with this autobiographical material: (1) Ezra Pound's marvelous mis-translation of a Chinese ideogram—"Sincerity...the sun's lance coming to rest on the precise spot verbally"...(of which I would change, for my pur-poses, the last word to "visually"), (2) Robert Creeley's trace-of-the-word for me on the back of a Buffalo restaurant menu—"Sym-keros...same-growth (Ceres) *create*...of the same growth," and (3) Hollis Frampton's track-of-it to "the greek, viz.—'a glazed pot' (i.e. one which will hold water)." This film might best be seen, then, as a graph of light equivalent to autobiographical thought process. 16mm, 27 min., color, silent.

Sincerity II *(1975)*

This continuation of my autobiography is composed of film photographed by many people: Bruce Baillie, Jane Brakhage, Larry Jordan and Stan Phillips, among others. Most of the footage is drawn from 20,000 feet of "home mov-ies," "out-takes" and the like, I've salvaged of my photography over the years. It is of the Brakhage family's coming into being. / It is composed in the light of those electrical traces we call "memory"; and it is as true to that "thought process" as I was enabled to make it. 16mm, 38.5 min., color, silent.

Sincerity III *(1978)*

In the autobiographical tradition of earlier Sincerities, this film takes up the light-threads of our living 14 years ago when the Brakhage family found Home and "settled," like they say, into some sense of permanence. This quality ofliv-mg in one place tends to destroy most senses of chronology: thus, along lines-of-thought of growing and shifting physicality, events *can* seem to be occurmg simultaneously (a thot-process 'kin to that of *The Domain of the Moment),* and the memory of such a time IS prompted and sustained by details ofliv- mg usually overlooked or taken- for-granted (such as Proust's cookie which prompted *Remembrance of Things Past).* Michael McClure's *Fleas* and Andrew Noren's *The Exquisite Corpse* hf were additional sources of inspira-tion for the making of this work. 16mm, 37.5 min., color, silent.

Sincerity IV *(1980)*

This, the 6th film of the Sincerity/ Duplicity series, seems rooted in the earli-est tradition of my work, Psycho- Drama, as well as in the most recent, Imagnostic, directions taken. It is remembrance as thought fashions it in lonely hotel rooms, sincere return of the mind to that which is loved, ephemeral faces of children growing older, familiar objects interwoven with easy alien famil-iarity, the images of strangers in UNeasy identification, sexual posture and the lure of The Beloved as irreducible image. 16mm, 37.5 min, color, silent.

Sincerity V *(1980)*

This, then, finishes eleven years of edit- mg drawing on 30-some years of photography. I will surely work autobiographically again, but the modes of "Sincerity and Duplicity" seem completed with this film which, on the one hand, is as simple in its integrity-of-light as those follow-the-ball "sing along" early silent movies and as complicated as teen-age metamorphosis. Childhood dissolves in flame, struck from the hearth. 16mm, 41 min., color, silent.

Sirius Remembered *(1959)*

I was coming to terms with decay of a dead thing and the decay of the memories of a loved being that had died and it was undermining all abstract concepts of death. The form was being cast out of probably the same physical need that makes dogs dance and howl in rhythm around a corpse. I was taking song as my source of inspiration for the rhythm structure, just as dogs dancing, prancing around a corpse, and howling in rhythm-structures or rhythm-intervals might be considered like thebirth of some kind of song. 16mm, 11 min., color, silent.

Skein *(1974)*

"A loosely coiled length of yarn (story)...wound on a reel" —my parenthesis! This is a painted film (inspired by Nolde's "unpainted pictures"): "skins" of paint hung in a weave of light. 16mm, 4.5 min., color, silent.

Sluice *(1978)*

It is a wooden silver-retrieving sluice, thus light-catch, awash with something like "cheek and jowl clippings ofArgentine bulls" (as Hollis Frampton reminds us) and many chemical residues of earth. My mind has grown TREE out of the forest of all of it. 16mm, 3.5 min., color, silent.

Soldiers and Other Cosmic Objects *(1977)*

This begins the 4th chapter of "The Book of The Film" and entertains directly the considerations of Chapter 2 *(The Weir Falcon Saga, The Machine of Eden,* and *The Animals of Eden and After). Person* begins to be defined by what it is *not.* It might be said that Chapter 1 *(Scenes From Under Childhood)* set forth birth and being, Chapter 2—consciousness, Chapter 3 *(Sincerity)—self-consciousness;* thus *Soldiers and Other Cosmic Objects* begins that strictly philosophical task of distinguishment (from, in this case, the rituals and trials of public school). I like to think of it as a work that Ludwig Wittgenstein might have found more than enjoyable. 16mm, 20.5 min., color, silent.

Star Garden *(1974)*

The "STAR," as it is singular, is the sun; and it is metaphored, at the beginning of this film, by the projector anyone uses to show it forth. Then the imaginary sun begins its course throughout whatever darkened room this film is seen within. At "high noon" (of the narrative) it can be imagined as if in back of the screen. Then it can be seen to shift its thought-light gradually back thru after-tones and imaginings of the "stars" of the film till it achieves a one-to-one relationship with moon again. This "sun" of the mind's eye of every viewer does only occasionally correspond with the off-screen "pictured sun" of the film; and anyone who cares to play this game of multiple illumination will surely see the film in its most completely conscious light. Otherwise it simply depicts (as Brancusi put it): "One of those days I would not trade for anything under heaven." 16mm, 22 min., color, silent.

The Stars Are Beautiful *(1975)*

This is the first sound film I've completed since 1962—the first sync sound ever. It is a philosophical film...extending the realm of *Blue Moses*. Its finest viewer, so far, has written: "The sun,—moon—and stars, really are the footprints of God.—/ "—and the broken fragments of the mirror that reflects reality.—/ "—and they are quite beautiful. I had not seen them before."— John Newell). 16mm, 19.5 min., color, sound.

Thigh Line Lyre Triangular *(1961)*

Only at a crisis do I see both the scene as I've been trained to see it (that is, with Renaissance perspective, three-dimensional logic—colors as we've been trained to call a color a color, and so forth) and patterns that move straight out from the inside of the mind through the optic nerves...spots before my eyes, so to speak...and it's a very intensive, disturbing, but joyful experience. I've seen that every time a child was born... Now none of that was in *Window Water Baby Moving;* and I wanted a childbirth film which expressed all of my seeing at such a time. 16mm, 17 min., color, silent.

Thot-Fal'n *(1978)*

This film describes a psychological state 'kin to "moon-struck," its images emblems (not quite symbols) of suspension-of-self within consciousness and then that feeling of "falling away" from conscious thought. The film can only be said to "describe" or be emblematic of this state because I cannot imagine symbolizing or otherwise representing an equivalent of thoughtlessness itself. Thus the "actors" in the film, Jane Brakhage, Tom and Gloria Bartek, William Burroughs, Allen Ginsberg, Peter Orlovsky and Phillip Whalen are figments of this Thought-Fallen PROCESS, as are their images in the film to themselves being photographed. 16mm, 10.5 min., color, silent.

23rd Psalm Branch: Part 1 *(1966-67,1978)*

This work, created in Reg. 8mm a decade ago, optically enlarged to 16mm, was in great danger (as all the *Songs*) of being lost forever due to deterioration of the Original and all Lab Masters. Despite great expense, I've managed to enlarge the Original (step-printed) into a 16mm Master. I chose this film (above all other *Songs)* FIRST because the multiple splices and hand-painted sections of it endangered it the most AND because I fear the war-inclination of this society at this time once again. P. Adams Sitney writes (in *Visionary Film):* "The furthest that Brakhage came in extending the language of 8mm cinema was his editing of the *23rd Psalm Branch*....The phenomenal and painstaking craftsmanship of this film reflects the intensity of the obsession with which its theme grasped his mind. In 1966, out of confusion about the Vietnam war and the American reaction to it, Brakhage began to meditate on the nature of war... The fruit of his studies and thoughts was the longest and most important of the *Songs*. ...it is an apocalypse of the imagination." 8mm and 16mm, 67 min., color, silent.

Visions in Meditation #1 *(1989)*

This is a film inspired by Gertrude Stein's "Stanzas in Meditation," in which the filmmaker has edited a meditative series of images of landscapes and human symbolism "indicative of that field-of-consciousness within which humanity survives thoughtfully." It is a film "as in a dream," this first film in a proposed series of such being composed of images shot in the New England states and Eastern Canada. It begins with an antique photograph of a baby and ends with a child loose on the landscape, interweaving images of Niagara Falls with a variety of New England and Eastern Canadian scenes, antique photographs, windows, old farms and cityscapes, as it moves from deep winter, through glare ice, to thaw. 16mm, 20 min., color, silent.

Visions in Meditation #2: Mesa Verde *(1989)*

This meditation takes its visual imperatives from the occasion of Mesa Verde, which I came to see finally as a Time rather than any such solidity as Place. "There is a terror here," were the first words which came to mind on seeing these ruins; and for two days after, during all my photography, I was haunted by some unknown occurrence which reverberated still in these rocks and rock-structures and environs. I can no longer believe that the Indians abandoned this solid habitation because of drought, lack-of-water, somesuch. (These explanations do not, anyway, account for the fact that all memory of The Place, *i.e.*, where it is, was eradicated from tribal memory, leaving only legend of a Time which such a place existed.) Midst the rhythms, then, of editing, I was compelled to introduce images which corroborate what the rocks said, and what the film strips seemed to say: The abandonment of the Mesa Verde was an eventuality (rather than an event), was for All Time thus, and had been intrinsic from the first such human building. 16mm, 17 min., color, silent.

Visions in Meditation #3: Plato's Cave *(1990)*

Plato's cave would seem to be the *idee fixe* of this film. The vortex would, then, be the phenomenological world—overwhelming, and thus "uninhabitable." The structures of thoughtful meditation are naturally, therefore, equivocal so that, for example, even a tornado-in-the-making will be both "dust devil" and "finger of God" at one with the clockwork sun and the strands of ice/fire, horizon, rock, clouds, so on.

The film is, I believe, a vision of mentality as most people must (to the irritation of Plato) have it, safely encaved and metaphorical, for the nervous system to survive. All the same I hope, with this work, to have brought a little "rush light" into the darkness. The film is set to the three movements of Rick

Corrigan's "Memory Suite." Its multiple superimpositions are superbly timed by Louise Fujiki, of Western Cine, as usual. 16 mm, 8 min., color.

The Weir-Falcon Saga *(1970)*
The Weir-Falcon Saga, The Machine of Eden, The Animals of Eden and After
The term *The Weir-Falcon Saga* appeared to me, night after night, at the end of each of a series of dreams: I was "true" to the feeling, tho' not the images, of those dreams in the editing of this and the following two films. The three films "go" very directly together, in the (above) order of their making: yet each seems to be a clear film in itself. At this time, I tend to think they constitute Chapter No. 2 of "The Book of The Film" I've had in mind these last five years (considering *Scenes From Under Childhood* as Chapter No. 1): and yet these "Weir-Falcon" films occur to me as distinct from any film-making I have done before. They engender, in me, entirely "new" considerations. I cannot describe them: but there is an excerpt from "The Spoils," by Basil Bunting, which raises hair on the back of my neck similarly: "Have you seen a falcon stoop/ accurate, unforseen/ and absolute, between/ wind-ripples over harvest? Dead/of what's to be, is and has been—/ were we not better dead?/ His wings churn air/ to flight./ Feathers alight/ with sun, he rises where/ dazzle rebuts our stare,/ wonder our fright." I might add that *The Machine (of Eden) operates* via "spots"—from sun's disks (of the camera lens) thru emulsion grains (within which, each, a universe might be found) and snow's flakes (echoing technical aberrations on film's surface) blots (upon the lens itself) and the circles of sun and moon, et cetera; these "mis-takes" give birth to "shape" (which, in this work, is "matter," subject and otherwise) amidst a weave of thought: (I add these technicalities, here, to help viewers defeat the habits of classical symbolism so that this work may be *immediately* seen, in its own light): the "dream" of Eden will speak for itself. 16mm, 35.5 min., color, silent.

The Wold Shadow *(1972)*
"Wold" because the word refers to 'forests' which poets later made "plains," and because the word also contains the rustic sense "to kill"—this then my laboriously painted vision of the god of the forest. 16mm, 3 min., color, silent.

Yggdrasill Whose Roots Are Stars in the Human Mind *(1997)*
This film, a combination of hand-painting and photography, is a fulsome exposition of the themes of *Dog Star Man*. In that early epic I had envisioned The World Tree as dead, fit only for firewood; and at end of *Dog Star Man* I had chopped it up amidst a flurry of stars (finally Cassiopia's Chair): now, these many years later, I am compelled to comprehend Yggrasill as rooted in the complex electrical synapses of thought process, to sense it being alive today as when nordic legendry hatched it. I share this compulsion with Andrei Tarkovsky, whose last film *The Sacrifice* struggles to review The World Tree narratively, whereas I simply present (one might almost say "document") a moving graph approximate to my thought process, whereby The Tree roots itself as the stars we, reflectively, are. 16mm, 17 min., color, silent.

selelcted bibliography

A complete bibliography through 1982 is available in Stan Brakhage: A Guide to References and Resources *by Gerald R. Barrett and Wendy Brabner, published by G.K. Hall and Co., 1983. The following selection of post-1982 citations was compiled by Marilyn Jull Brakhage.*

Abbot, M.B. "Hidden Treasure," *Boulder Planet,* Vol.111, No. 28, January 13-19, 1999, pp. 27, 30.

Anker, Steve. "The Avant-Garde into the Eighties," *Independent America: New Film 1978-1988.* American Museum of the Moving Image, Oct 7–Nov 11, 1988, pp. 9-15.

Arthur, Paul. "The God of Day Had Gone Down Upon Him," *Film Comment,* May/June, 2000, p. 72.

Belnap, Gillian, ed. *Carnegie Museum of Art: Collection Highlights.* Pittsburgh, Penn.: Carnegie Museum of Art, 1995. Images from "Dog Star Man" on p. 71, back cover.

Brakhage, Jane. "The Autobiography of Stan Brakhage" (chapters 1-4), *Motion Picture,* Vol. 1, No. 1, Spring/Summer 1986, pp. 1-20; No. 2, Fall 1986, pp. 8-11; No. 3, Spring 1987, pp. 8-9.

Brakhage, Stan, and Williams, Forrest. "On Filming Light," *The Structurist,* 13/14, 1973/74, pp. 90-100.

Brakhage, Stan. "The Swiftly Perceived Blur," *Rolling Stock,* No. 1, Summer, 1980, pp. 10, 11, 16.

_____. "Brakhage at the Ninth Telluride," *Rolling Stock,* No. 4, 1983, pp.18-19.

_____. "Brakhage Pans Telluride Gold," *Rolling Stock,* No. 6, 1983, pp.11-14.

_____. "Telluride Zinc," *Rolling Stock,* No. 8, 1984, pp. 24-26.

_____. "Letter to Jack Chambers" and "Letter to Edith," *The Capilano Review,* No. 33, 1984, pp. 42-3.

_____. "Telluride Takes," *Rolling Stock,* No. 11, 1986, pp. 9-11.

_____. "Brakhage Observes Telluride the 13th," *Rolling Stock,* No. 12, 1986, pp. 29-31.

_____. "Stan Brakhage at the Millennium: November 4, 1977," *Millennium Film Journal,* 16/17/18, Fall/Winter 1986-87, pp. 297-307.

_____. "The 'Song' of El Paso," *Super 8mm: The Last Frontier.* Manchester, N.H.: Cunier Gallery of Art. Spring 1987, pp.12-13.

_____. "James Tenney," *Perspectives of New Music,* Vol. 25, 1987.

_____. "Some Words on the North," *American Book Review,* Vol 10, No.2, May-June 1988, pp. 5-18.

_____. "Time...on dit," *Musicworks.* A quarterly column in this Canadian journal appeared from 1990-1999 in Nos. 45, 47-50, 52-73.

_____. "Gertrude Stein: Meditative Literature and Film," *Council on Research and Creative Work Distinguished Lecture Series,* The Graduate School, University of Colorado at Bouder, Fall 1990.

_____. "Stan Brakhage on Marie Menken," *Film Culture*, No.78, Summer, 1994, pp. 1-9. Transcript of a lecture delivered at the Innis Film Society, Toronto, Nov.. 19, 1992.

_____. In "A Film Comment Poll," *Film Comment*, Jan./Feb. 2000, p. 54.

Bromfield, David. "The Most Natural Thing," *in picture: Western Australia's Independent Film and Video Magazine*, October 1994, pp. 6-8.

Camper, Fred. "A Musical Way of Seeing," *Chicago Reader*, April 16, 1993, pp. 16, 31.

_____. "Glimpses of Greatness, New Films by Stan Brakhage," *Chicago Reader*, Sept. 10,1999, pp. 44-46.

_____. "Sanitized for Our Protection." A review of the films *Brakhage*, directed by Jim Shedden, and *Reichstag*, directed by Jorg Daniel and Wolfran Hissen. *Chicago Reader*, Dec. 3, 1999, pp. 44-46.

Davenport, Guy. *The Geography of the Imagination: Forty Essays*. San Francisco: North Point Press, 1981.

Dorsky, Nathaniel. "Stan Brakhage: Four Silent Nights," University Art Museum Newspaper of Univ. of Calif., Berkeley, July-August 1994, p. 6.

Elder, Bruce. *Image and Identity: Reflections on Canadian Film and Culture*. Waterloo, Ontario: Wilfrid Laurier University Press, 1989.

_____. *The Body in Film*. Toronto: Art Gallery of Ontario, 1991.

_____. *A Body of Vision*. Waterloo, Ontario: Wilfrid Laurier Univ.. Press, 1997.

_____. *The Films of Stan Brakhage in the American Tradition of Ezra Pound, Gertrude Stein, and Charles Olson*. Waterloo, Ontario: Wilfrid Laurier Univ.. Press, 1998.

Field, Simon. "In the American Vein: Stan Brakhage since the 60's," *Monthly Film Bulletin of The British Film Institute*, Vol. 53, No. 625, Feb. 1986, pp. 60-62.

_____. "Creation," *Monthly Film Builetin of The British Film Institute*, Vol. 53, No. 626, March 1986, pp. 93-94.

_____. "Scenes From Under Childhood—Section 1," *Monthly Film Bulletin of The British Film Institute*, Vol. 53, No. 626, March 1986, p. 94.

Foye, Raymond, ed. *Phiilp Taaffe: Composite Nature (A Conversation with Stan Brakhage)*. New York: Peter Blum, Blumarts Inc., 1997.

Ganguly, Suranjan. "All That is is Light: Brakhage at Sixty," *Sight and Sound*, October 1993, pp. 20-23.

_____. "Stan Brakhage—The 60th Birthday Interview," *Film Culture*, No. 78, Summer 1994, pp. 18-38.

Grimes, William. "In Film's Avant-Garde for 40 Years," *New York Times*, Feb.6,1993, p. 9.

Hoberman, J. "Blast from the Past: Stan Brakhage's Child's Garden and the Serious Sea," *The Village Voice*, Feb. 9, 1993, p. 53.

Jacobs, Ken. In "A Film Comment Poll," *Film Comment*, Jan./Feb. 2000, p. 56.

James, David E. *Allegories of Cinema: American Film in the Sixties*. Princeton: Princeton University Press, 1989.

Janik, David. "A Semi-Formal Affair: Brakhage Screens Four Films and Receives Honorary Degree," *The Bard Observer*, Vol. 10, No. 7, Apr. 10, 2000, p. 2

Jenkins, Bruce. "Stan Brakhage: The Art of Seeing," *Walker Art Center,* 1999.

Keller, Marjorie. *The Untutored Eye: Childhood in the Films of Cocteau, Cornell and Brakhage.* London and Toronto: Associated University Presses, 1986.

Kelly, Robert. "Brakhage, The Autonomous." Bard College program catalogue, March 28, 2000, pp. 2-3.

Kertess, Klaus, ed. *Catalogue for the Biennial Exhibition of the Whitney Museum of American Art.* New York: Harry N. Abrams, Inc., 1995, pp. 76, 77.

Luna, Chris. "The Films of Stan Brakhage in the American Tradition of Ezra Pound, Gertrude Stein, and Charles Olson," *Rain Taxi review of books,* Vol. 4, No. 4, Winter 1999/2000, pp. 22-23.

Mason, Marilynne. "Stan Brakhage's Last Interview," *Northern Lights: Studies in Creativity,* ed. Stanley Scott. Univ. of Maine at Presque Isle, 1983; pp. 7-33.

Mast, Gerald and Kawin, Bruce. *A Short History of the Movies.* Needham Heights, Mass.: Allyn and Bacon, 1996. Esp. pp. 498-9.

Mast, Gerald and Cohen, Marshall and Braudy, Leo. *Film Theory and Criticism, 4th Edition.* New York, Oxford: Oxford University Press, 1992, pp.71-78.

Michelson, Peter. *Speaking the Unspeakable: A Poetics of Obscenity.* New York: State University of New York Press, 1993. Chapter 9, pp. 223-274.

Morgan, Robert C. "Light Years Ahead: Stan Brakhage," *NY Arts (International Edition),* Vol. 5, No. 3, March 2000, pp. 16-17.

Moshovitz, Howie. "Avant-Garde Focus Softens for Brakhage," *Denver Post,* Jan. 17, 1993, section E, p. 1.

O'Pray, Michael. "Sincerity Reels 1,2,3," *Monthly Film Bulletin of The British Film Institute,* Vol. 53, No. 625, February 1986, p. 63.

Pruitt, John. "Stan Brakhage: An Appreciation." Bard College program catalogue, March 28, 2000, pp. 4-8.

Rees, A.L. "Murder Psalm," *Monthly Film Bulletin of The British Film Institute,* Vol.53, No.625 (February 1986), p. 63.

_____. "Tortured Dust" and "Unconscious London Strata," *Monthly Film Bulletin of The British Film Institute,* Vol. 53, No. 626, March 1986, pp.86-87 and pp. 94-95.

Rosenbaum, Jonathan. "The Act of Seeing with one's own eyes," *Monthly Film Bulletin of The British Film Institute,* Vol. 53, No. 625, Feb. 1986, p. 62.

Sharrett, Christopher. "Brakhage's Scrapbook," *Millennium Film Journal,* 14/15, Fall/Winter 1984-85, pp. 23-27.

Solomon, Deborah. *Utopia Parkway, The Life and Work of Joseph Cornell.* New York: Farrar, Straus and Giroux, 1997.

Sterritt, David. "To Capture the Flow of Thought," *The Christian Science Monitor* (April 20, 1993), p.13.

Wees, William C. *Light Moving in Time.* Berkeley: Univ. of Calif. Press, 1992.

White, Jerry. "Cinema Brakhage," *Telluride Daily Planet,* Sept. 1, 2000, p. 42.

Wilkens, John. "Brakhage: Cinematic Dream Catcher," *Coloradan,* May 2000, pp.,14-15.